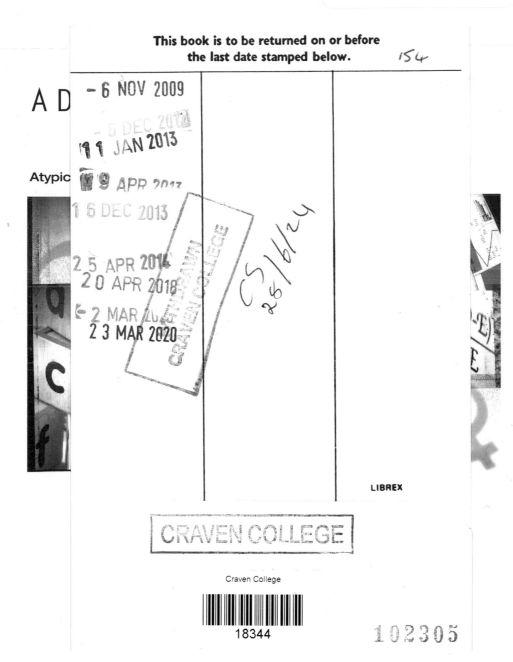

A D

Atypic

£9-99

ADVANCED PSYCHOLOGY

Atypical Behaviour

Lynda Turner

Hodder & Stoughton

A MEMBER OF THE HODDER HEADLINE GROUP

Orders: please contact Bookpoint Ltd, 130 Milton Park, Abingdon, Oxon OX14 4SB.
Telephone: (44) 01235 827720. Fax: (44) 01235 400454. Lines are open from 9.00 – 6.00,
Monday to Saturday, with a 24 hour message answering service. You can also order through our website
www.hodderheadline.co.uk.

British Library Cataloguing in Publication Data
A catalogue record for this title is available from the British Library

ISBN 0 340 859334

First Published 2003
Impression number 10 9 8 7 6 5 4 3 2 1
Year   2009 2008 2007 2006 2005 2004 2003

Typeset by Dorchester Typesetting Group Ltd, Dorchester, Dorset
Printed in Great Britain for Hodder & Stoughton Educational, a division of Hodder Headline Plc,
338 Euston Road, London NW1 3BH by J.W. Arrowsmith Ltd, Bristol

In memory of Leonard Waywell

The author and publishers would like to thank the following for permission to reproduce material in this book:

Figure 1.2 Mary Evans Picture Library; Figure 1.3 CORBIS/Ethan Miller; Figure 1.5 CORBIS/Jose Luis Pelaez, Inc.; Figure 2.1 CORBIS; Figure 2.3 Science Photo Library; Figure 2.5 CORBIS; Figure 2.8 CORBIS/Lawrence Manning; Figure 3.1 MIND; Figure 3.2 CORBIS/C.B.P. Photoproductions; Figure 3.3a EMPICS/Gabriel Piko; Figure 3.3b EMPICS/Tony Marshall; Figure 3.4 BFI; Figure 4.2 CORBIS/Jim Sugar Photography; Figure 4.6 Science Photo Library/John Greim; Figure 4.8 Science Photo Library; Figure 4.10 CORBIS/Jose Luis Pelaez, Inc.

While every effort has been made to trace copyright holders, this has not been possible in all cases; any omissions brought to our attention will be remedied in future printings.

Contents

How to use this book

This book has been designed to meet the needs of students and teachers studying for the Atypical Behaviour option from Module 4 of the AQA A2 level (Specification B) in Psychology.

Each chapter in this book provides short descriptions of empirical studies and experiments directly relating to the topic areas. There are also some small group and individual activities to try. It is recommended that you carry out as many of these as possible since they will help you with remembering material and thinking more deeply and critically about psychology. The chapters offer numerous evaluative comments that will help you to analyse, discuss and make application of theory, concepts and research. This will help you gain AO2 marks (for evaluation and application) in the examination.

Each chapter contains four different types of learning activities as follows:

Reflective Activity This invites you to engage in a reflective activity. This gives you something to think about before continuing with your reading.

Practical Activity This invites you to conduct some kind of practical activity. Here a suggestion is made that may be carried out either on your own or with a small group of people. Some activities will take time outside of reading further in the chapter.

Study This indicates that a study or experiment in psychology is described. Studies have been selected that are important and/or highlight theory or key concepts in psychology. The study or experiment is presented in the way required when you are asked to describe a study in an examination question. When reading the study try to identify strengths and shortcomings, and think about ways in which the study could be improved.

Evaluative Comment This indicates an evaluative comment. These provide you with critical comment and analysis. Try to elaborate on the point being made, or use the comment as a basis for a small group discussion to explore other points of view. The skills of evaluation and analysis are essential to the study of psychology and are needed if you wish to gain high grades. Evaluative comments help with the second assessment objective (AO2) examined throughout the AS and A level in psychology.

Towards the end of each chapter you will find a number of questions. These have been set in the style that appears in the AQA Specification B A2 examinations. Each question shows the number of marks available and the marks for the two assessment objectives. Assessment Objective 1 (AO1) is concerned with knowledge and understanding. Assessment Objective 2 (AO2) is concerned with critical evaluation, analysis and application of psychology.

At the end of each chapter you will find suggestions for further reading. This is given in two parts, first introductory books and then more specialist texts. The introductory texts should be easily accessible to all students. The specialist books are more demanding and will be of value to students who wish to achieve high grades. Some relevant and accessible websites are also provided.

I hope you enjoy reading this book!

Acknowledgements

I would like to thank Julie McLoughlin for the encouragement to give it a go, and Donald Pennington for his patience in editing this text. Special thanks go to my family, Alma, Jack, Mark, Angela, Michael and Clare Turner for copious tea and sympathy. I will not mention 'the book' again! Finally, I am very grateful for the support of my friends, including Christine Collister, Helen Watson, Collete O'Neil, Christine Davies, Dave Berry, Jane Sisk and especially Lynn Johnson, who had a development project of her own going on at the same time: the very beautiful baby Samuel.

Lynda Turner

March 2003

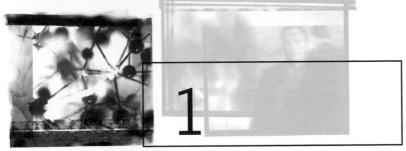

Definition and classification of atypical behaviour

1.1 Introduction

Most people have questioned their own and other people's thoughts, feelings and behaviour at some time or another. It isn't always easy to explain why someone responds in a particular way. For example, loyal football fans often continue to attend matches, despite their team frequently being defeated. They do not enjoy watching the game each week but feel compelled to do so. Why do they do it? Other people find it difficult to understand why anyone would choose to spend their Saturday afternoons watching a group of men kick a ball around a field!

It is even more complicated to try to explain behaviour that is unexpected or bizarre, such as an individual shouting at an imaginary companion. **Atypical psychology** is concerned with behaviour that is unusual, that is not typical of an ordinary person. It involves examining the possible causes and treatments of mental health problems. Some psychological difficulties are quite common, such as depression. Many of us will experience, or have experienced, a period of doubt and unhappiness. Other disorders occur less frequently, with long-term effects, such as schizophrenia. Individuals with schizophrenia sometimes hear voices in their heads and lose touch with reality. Atypical (or abnormal) psychology is one of the most popular options in undergraduate courses (Davison and Neale, 2001) and is often what attracts people to study psychology in the first place. It is a fascinating area but one that is fraught with difficulties and controversy.

1.2 Historical ideas of abnormality

In early ancient cultures, behaviour that appeared beyond the control of an individual was explained by **demonology** (Davison and Neale, 2001). This is the belief that an evil spirit, such as the devil, had taken over the mind and body of the sufferer. Treatment would involve rituals – such as chanting or praying – or more aggressive behaviour such as beating or starving the individual. The process is known as exorcism. The aim of exorcism was to force the evil spirits out of the sufferer's body.

Hippocrates (460–377 BC) is regarded as the founder of medicine and the first to regard mental illness as a disease with natural causes. He saw the importance of the brain in consciousness, intelligence and emotion. Hippocrates divided mental disorders into three categories: mania, melancholia and brain fever. His system can be seen as a very early and much simpler classification system than the one currently used today. He suggested very different treatment to exorcism, such as rest, peaceful surroundings and a good diet. Unfortunately, his understanding of the structure of normal brain functioning was completely inaccurate. He believed that mental health was dependent on four fluids in the body known as humours. An imbalance of these fluids, it was thought, produced disorders. (For an example of these humours and their effect see Figure 1.1.) Hippocrates was one of the earliest practitioners to believe in physical causes for mental ill health, which is known as **somatogenesis**.

The humour (bodily fluid)	Effect of an imbalance
Phlegm	Dull and lacking energy
Blood	Mood swings and a changeable temperament
Black bile	Melancholia (depressive symptoms)
Yellow bile	Irritability and anxiety

Figure 1.1: Examples of the four Hippocratic humours

The progressive and humane view of mental illness did not continue and throughout the Middle Ages a belief in demonology returned. Seriously disturbed individuals were thought to possess supernatural powers that could cause harm to others. As a result there was an increase in violence and mistrust towards them, often ending in a trial for witchcraft. Historians have documented that many thousands of people were executed during this time for allegedly practising witchcraft. Among those killed were the mentally disturbed.

In the latter part of the Middle Ages the first **asylums** were created. These were buildings specifically used to house and care for the mentally ill. Early asylums were no better than prisons. The inmates were kept in filthy cells and treated more like animals than humans. The Priory of St Mary of Bethlehem in London was one of these early asylums and became a great tourist attraction. Tickets were sold to view the violent patients, and the mentally ill became a source of entertainment. The term **bedlam** (slang for Bethlehem) has since become associated with a place of extreme confusion and uproar. Some of the treatments devised at this time were no better than earlier efforts. For example, Deutsch (1949) describes a commonly held view that 'lunatics' could be cured by extreme fear. One doctor had a coffin-like box for the patient, with holes drilled in it. The box was lowered into a tank of cold water and kept there until air bubbles stopped coming to the surface of the water. Many patients did not survive this treatment. It seems no different in principle than the ducking stool, used to determine whether someone was a witch in the early Middle Ages.

Phillipe Pinel (1745–1826) is considered to be the first humanitarian practitioner in asylums for the mentally ill. He was in charge of a large institution in Paris and was determined to treat the inmates as individual and sick human beings rather than animals. He removed their chains and shackles, and allowed them to walk around the hospital grounds. Many patients who had been uncontrollable became calm and easier to manage. Pinel's methods, sometimes referred to as **moral treatment**, can be seen as a return to ancient Hippocratic ideals, sadly lost for many centuries. In England, the York Retreat was established by William Tuke in 1796. He provided a quiet religious atmosphere for the mentally ill in the grounds of a country estate. Patients

A treatment method used in early asylums

could work in the gardens and take walks through the countryside. Attendants looked after them and talked with them about their difficulties.

As attitudes towards mental health changed, it became apparent that mental health disorders were more common than had previously been acknowledged. Major building programmes were undertaken in Europe and America to create large state-run asylums. These hospitals were responsible for the treatment of hundreds of patients. The intensive nature of moral treatment was unmanageable with such large numbers and the approach fell out of favour.

In the early twentieth century, there was also a return to somatogenesis, as knowledge and understanding of human physiology increased. For example, a physical cause had been discovered for a common mental disorder known as **general paresis**. The venereal disease syphilis was found to cause a gradual decline in mental and physical health, leading to the **delusions** and **hallucinations** of general paresis, followed, ultimately, by death. Prior to this discovery, about 10 per cent of inmates in asylums were diagnosed with the disorder. It is extremely rare today, due to the effectiveness of antibiotics in treating early symptoms of syphilis.

Physicians, most notably Kraeplin (1896), began documenting symptoms that regularly appeared together in different mental health problems. These are known as **syndromes**. Kraeplin proposed that the existence of syndromes suggested a different underlying physical cause for each distinct mental disorder documented. This was the beginning of the 'medical approach' and the concept of mental 'illness'. Kraeplin proposed two major groups of mental illness: **dementia praecox**, which was an early term for schizophrenia, and manic depressive psychosis, which is now known as bipolar mood disorder. He believed that a chemical imbalance caused dementia praecox, an idea that is still under investigation (see Chapter 3). An irregular metabolism was thought to cause **manic depressive** psychosis. Kraeplin's method of classifying disorders became the basis for the system in use today.

At the same time, a school of thought was emerging that attempted to understand mental disturbance in terms of psychological factors. Sigmund Freud studied a number of mentally disturbed individuals who had physical complaints, such as blindness, without any obvious cause. This led him to develop a theory based on **psychogenesis**, which is the belief that something is caused by psychological rather than physical factors. Later psychological approaches such as behaviourism, humanism and the cognitive school also supported psychogenesis.

The debate surrounding the psychogenic or somatogenic origins of mental illness remains today and is more commonly known as the mind–body debate (see Chapter 11 in *Advanced Psychology*). The work of mental health practitioners has also been divided between these two camps. The differences can be seen in the treatment methods and language used within each profession. Psychiatrists are medically trained doctors who have chosen to specialise in mental 'illness'. They adopt a somatogenic approach and believe physical 'treatments' such as antipsychotic drugs should be prescribed to 'patients'. Psychologists, on the other hand, are people who have a postgraduate degree in psychology and favour a psychogenic approach. They are more likely to use psychological interventions such as behavioural or cognitive 'therapy' (see Chapter 4) with 'clients'. Clinical psychologists are trained in assessment and diagnosis within the hospital environment but are not qualified to prescribe drugs. While, historically, there has been conflict between these two schools of thought, many practitioners today would favour an **interactionist** approach, combining both psychological and physiological knowledge and understanding.

As a result of developments in somatogenic treatments in the 1950s and 1960s, such as antidepressant and antipsychotic drugs, the need for large mental hospitals to house long-stay patients was significantly reduced. During the 1980s many specialist psychiatric hospitals were closed and **community care** was introduced. Patients now often receive treatment and care as out-patients, with regular appointments to see either a clinical psychologist or a psychiatrist. Alternatively, a community psychiatric nurse can visit people in their own homes (see Chapter 3).

REFLECTIVE Activity

Try to come up with your own definition of 'normal' and 'abnormal' behaviour. Compare your definition with those of other students in your class. You may want to refer back to your definitions once you have read the next section.

1.3 Definitions of abnormality

Psychologists and psychiatrists are involved in the day-to-day care and treatment of people with a variety of mental health problems, whose behaviour is described as abnormal. However, it is not easy to define exactly what is meant by abnormal (or atypical) behaviour.

Statistical infrequency

Abnormal behaviour could be defined as behaviour that is statistically infrequent in society. This approach is most useful when dealing with human characteristics that can be reliably measured, such as height. Most people's scores will cluster around the average, with fewer very small or tall people. This is known as normal distribution. Gathering data about mental health problems is common. For example, anorexia is known to affect 1 per cent of the population, whereas bulimia affects 3 per cent (see Chapter 3). Both behaviours are therefore statistically infrequent. The approach is easy to understand and assumes that normal behaviour is 'average' behaviour.

EVALUATIVE COMMENT
PRACTICAL PROBLEMS
To ensure that behaviour is statistically infrequent requires the collection and maintenance of accurate data about the population as a whole. This would be a time-consuming and extremely complex task. Also, researchers would have to agree on how 'infrequent' a behaviour should be for a definition of abnormality.
ETHICAL DILEMMAS
The approach does not differentiate between what is statistically infrequent and yet valued in

society (such as musical talent) and behaviour that is undesirable (such as murderous rage). Also, many people suffer from depression. Those who seek help from a professional clearly see their own behaviour as abnormal, although it is not statistically infrequent.

Violation of social norms

A second approach involves considering behaviour that differs from the usual (or norm) in society. It introduces the concept of what is desirable and expected behaviour in different circumstances and situations. A **situational norm** dictates what kind of behaviour is acceptable in a given situation. For example, stripping naked is acceptable in the shower room but not in the gym. A **developmental norm** indicates the kind of behaviour that is acceptable at a certain age. For example, young children can cry loudly when they are bored, but A-level students cannot! Abnormal behaviour is therefore defined as any behaviour that transgresses social norms.

EVALUATIVE COMMENT

PRACTICAL PROBLEMS

The definition is too broad and would include behaviours that are against social norms but are not universally considered to be abnormal, such as smoking. Social norms also change over time. For example, it is much less socially acceptable to smoke cigarettes today than it was 20 years ago. Smoking was allowed on public transport and in cinemas and the workplace. Definitions of atypical behaviour would have to be constantly revised to keep up with changes in social norms.

Also, many people with mental health problems are not obviously breaking any social norms. For example, someone with a phobia of heights is unlikely to behave in an unlawful or undesirable way.

ETHICAL DILEMMAS

A major difficulty with this approach is that it defines anyone who goes against social norms as abnormal and therefore mentally disturbed. People could be defined as abnormal because of their sexual preferences, religious beliefs or political ideas. For example, homosexuality was defined as a mental illness until 1973. Social pressure, from many professionals in the field of mental health and gay activists, was needed to change the definition.

Some researchers believe that adherence to social norms can actually create mental health problems. For example, the incidence of anorexia among young women (see Chapter 2) has been linked to the social pressure to be thin.

Musical talent is infrequent but socially valued

REFLECTIVE Activity

Think of three situational norms that would operate on a psychiatric ward. For example, staff would be expected to buy their own lunch, whereas patients are provided for. How would these norms affect the behaviour, thoughts and feelings of staff and patients?

Different subcultures operate in every college

Cultural differences

The term **culture** means a set of values, beliefs and attitudes shared by most members of a community. An i n d i v i d u a l ' s behaviour is governed to some extent by the culture he or she lives in. What may be acceptable in one culture could be perceived as a severe social problem in another. For example, voice-hearing is an acceptable part of some religious faiths, yet is perceived, among the psychiatric community, as a symptom of mental illness. Behaviour can be perceived as abnormal, when in fact it is simply culturally different and normal to that culture.

Kaiser *et al.* (1998) claim that psychiatrists are now encouraged to be aware of cultural differences when assessing patients. The manual they use to diagnose mental health problems (see Section 1.5) outlines conditions that appear most often in specific cultures, as well as some cultural variations in the way symptoms are described. For example, in some cultures, depression is expressed as a physical pain, other cultures describe depression as a feeling, such as sadness.

EVALUATIVE COMMENT

PRACTICAL PROBLEMS

Developing detailed knowledge of other cultural groups would be highly time consuming. Within each culture there are a number of subcultures, which are any section of society holding different views and attitudes to the dominant culture. For example, younger people may have a different set of attitudes to older members in society. As cultures and subcultures also develop and change over time, maintaining knowledge would be a very complex, ongoing process.

ETHICAL DILEMMAS

Attempting to define abnormality is in itself a culturally specific task, centred as it is on the notion of mental health care professionals who diagnose and treat 'patients'. Other cultures may be more accepting and tolerant of unusual behaviour within their society. For example, Lin and Kleinman (1988) found that non-industrialised societies had higher recovery rates for people displaying symptoms of schizophrenia. They believed this was because the social environment was more supportive and allowed people to recover at their own pace.

Research has cast doubt on whether awareness of cultural differences has contributed to making an accurate diagnosis, as Kaiser *et al.* (1998) claimed.

Study 1.1

AIM Lopez and Hernandez (1986) wanted to investigate the effectiveness of being aware of cultural diversity when making a mental health diagnosis.

METHOD They surveyed a large sample of mental health practitioners in California, who were trying to avoid discrimination against minority groups by being culturally aware. They looked at clinical assessments and treatments offered to patients over a period of time.

RESULT Many practitioners minimised the seriousness of patients' problems by assuming their behaviour was culturally different rather than abnormal. For example, one clinician claimed that an African-American woman, who was suffering from symptoms of schizophrenia, did not require treatment. He believed that hallucinations were a normal part of African-American culture.

CONCLUSION Sensitivity about cultural diversity may reduce the chances of some cultural groups receiving appropriate treatment.

REFLECTIVE Activity

There will be many subcultures operating within your college or school. For example, not everybody will agree on the social value of the singers shown on page 5! List five different social groups and indicate a behaviour within each group that could be seen as abnormal by outsiders.

Distress

Many people with mental health problems experience intense unhappiness and anxiety. Sometimes psychological problems can cause physical complaints, and patients visit their doctor believing they are physically unwell. Rather than labelling an individual's behaviour as statistically infrequent or socially undesirable, abnormality could be defined as thoughts, feelings or behaviours that distress the individual. This seems a kinder definition because it includes the experiences of the individual sufferer. The approach also acknowledges the need for treatments to alleviate personal distress.

EVALUATIVE COMMENT

PRACTICAL PROBLEMS

There has been a practical difficulty in producing a reliable way of measuring distress. Each individual may show and experience their distress in different ways. For example, a highly disturbed individual may choose to withdraw and not report distress, while another person might react by attempting suicide.

ETHICAL DILEMMAS

Some mental health problems do not cause distress to the individual. For example, during the manic phase of bipolar disorder, the patient can feel marvellous and strongly resist any attempt at treatment (see Chapter 3). This type of disorder is called a psychosis. The sufferer has a severe mental disturbance that has seriously impaired their emotional responses and thought processes. The individual may be in need of help and protection, despite a lack of any obvious distress.

An alternative view could consider the amount of distress caused to other people by the individual's unusual behaviour. For example, anorexic patients are often brought to the attention of professionals by deeply concerned parents. Using this approach, treatment can be given to patients who might otherwise resist it, or deny they have a problem.

REFLECTIVE Activity

There is an ethical dilemma in using distress caused to others as an indicator of abnormality. List five behaviours that are common in your age group, which can cause distress to others. List some people who may be distressed by these behaviours. Compare your list with that of another student. How abnormal are these behaviours? Who says so?

Maladaptiveness

Another way of defining abnormality is to look at the consequences for the individual. Adaptive behaviour is that which enables an individual to thrive in their environment.

Mental health problems can seriously affect all aspects of an individual's life. They can disrupt social relationships, work, academic study and the ability to achieve personal goals. Abnormality can therefore be defined as **maladaptiveness**, where the thoughts, feelings and behaviour experienced interfere with progress in the world.

EVALUATIVE COMMENT
PRACTICAL PROBLEMS
This definition could be applied to all of us at some point in our lives. For example, excessive partying during an A-level course is likely to affect the overall grades achieved. Maladaptiveness can perhaps be accepted as normal behaviour at certain stages in our lives. This creates the problem of trying to decide how much maladaptiveness is too much.
ETHICAL DILEMMAS
The main difficulty with this approach is whether or not the patient, their family or a mental health practitioner is responsible for defining maladaptiveness. For example, a person may want to lead a very isolated and secluded existence. The definition assumes that there is a 'normal' way of living, excluding individual choice to live outside the mainstream.

Also, some mental health problems cause personal distress to the individual, without having terrible consequences. For example, claustrophobia (a fear of enclosed spaces) may cause an individual to seek treatment although the behaviour does not have a major impact on their work, social or personal life.

PRACTICAL Activity

Look at the different types of behaviour listed in Figure 1.5. Decide whether you would consider each of them:

1. statistically infrequent

2. violation of social norms

3. cultural difference

4. sign of distress

5. maladaptiveness.

1.4 Diagnosis and classification

The medical model

The best-known explanation for abnormality in our culture is the medical model. Mental disorders are regarded as 'illnesses' caused by biological factors such as infection, genetics, brain chemistry or brain damage. For example, in Alzheimer's disease, the brain tissue irreversibly deteriorates, initially causing difficulty with concentration and memory. As the

Type of behaviour	Definition – infrequent/violation of social norms/culturally different/ distress/maladaptiveness
1. Having size 14 feet	
2. Pushing needles repeatedly into your skin to leave a permanent scar	
3. Believing that aliens are working with the government	
4. Missing college and work as a result of smoking too much cannabis	
5. Lying down in the street	
6. Feeling very unhappy and wanting to die	
7. Standing in the middle of a field singing loudly and dancing frantically	
8. Cutting your face open and rubbing ash into the wounds	
9. Drinking two bottles of vodka a day	
10. Writing a piano concerto at the age of three	

Figure 1.5: Types of behaviour

illness progresses, the personality of the sufferer is affected and they begin to display psychological disturbance. This type of mental illness is known as an **organic disorder** because it has a clear physical cause. Autopsies of Alzheimer's patients show consistently similar physiological changes in the brain.

Clear biological causes of other mental disorders, such as anorexia nervosa (see Chapter 2) have yet to be identified. These types of illness are known as **functional disorders**. There is no demonstrable physical cause but something has gone wrong with the way the person functions (or acts) in the world. Many psychiatrists believe that medical science will eventually identify the physical causes of functional disorders.

The main practitioners in the somatogenic approach are **psychiatrists**. They are medical doctors who have specialised in the area of mental health. Psychiatrists work in hospitals, can give physical examinations, and diagnose both mental and physical illness. They also decide on what medical treatment is needed. A psychiatrist can prescribe drugs, **electro convulsive therapy (ECT)** and, in extreme cases, brain surgery (see Chapter 4).

Many patients (and their families) take comfort from the idea that their difficulties are due to biological factors beyond their control. The medical model means that the individual is not held personally responsible for their abnormal behaviour. The approach can be seen as a more caring and humane definition of abnormality, with a blameless victim who requires care and treatment. However, there are also some difficulties.

EVALUATIVE COMMENT
PRACTICAL PROBLEMS
The medical model presents a practical difficulty in diagnosing mental health problems. Identification is largely dependent on the interpretation of the individual patient's symptoms. With physical illness, the patient can describe symptoms – for example, a pain in the foot – and

the doctor can observe a physical sign: a swollen ankle. Objective medical tests, such as x-rays, can be undertaken to establish the condition of the patient. With mental 'illness', there are often no physical signs of any disease and critics of the approach would argue that some form of subjective (or value) judgement is made.

ETHICAL PROBLEMS

On the basis that mental illness can lead to a loss of control and responsibility, the Mental Health Act 1983 allows for the compulsory detention and treatment of the mentally ill if they represent a danger to themselves or others (see Chapter 4). The sick individual can get treatment and support, and will be closely monitored. However, critics from the anti-psychiatry movement (see below) have argued that this loss of rights is unethical and leads to discriminatory practice.

The medical model and social norms

In the 1960s a new school of thought developed known as the anti-psychiatry movement. Szasz (1962) was a major critic of the medical model. He claimed that, as there were no physical signs of brain disease in many disorders, it was inaccurate to describe 'problems in living' as mental illness. Szasz thought the medical definition of mental illness was flawed, just as earlier ideas of demonology were. The concept of 'illness' or 'demons' existed because the prevailing culture accepted it as a valid explanation, without any real evidence to support it. In the Middle Ages, people who deviated from social norms were tried and punished for witchcraft. In the twentieth century, psychiatry labelled them 'insane' and excluded them from society by sending them to a mental institution. Szasz therefore saw medical treatment as another form of punishment for those who would not conform to social norms.

Some medical treatments for mental health problems in the 1960s were undertaken with aggressive people who violated social norms. For example, Taylor (1992) reports that 38 000 leucotomies were undertaken in 1968, compared to just 18 in 1991. A **leucotomy** is a surgical procedure that involves cutting away the brain tissue connecting the frontal lobes. It causes permanent changes in behaviour, including intellectual impairment, lack of energy, personality changes and in some cases death. The main advantage of psychosurgery was that it made patients much easier to control. Many o these operations were undertaken without the consent of the patients, because they were believed to be incapable of making decisions for themselves.

In England and Wales, the use of psychosurgery is now governed by the Mental Health Act (1983). It can only be undertaken as a last resort and with the patient's consent. The work of Szasz and other members of the anti-psychiatry movement has contributed to a change in social norms surrounding the care and treatment of people with mental health problems.

The medical model and cultural differences

As Stirling and Hellewell (1999) point out, many psychiatrists in the UK are middle class, male and white. Mental health practitioners are therefore likely to be subject to their own **cultural bias**. This means that people tend to favour their own view of the world and perceive alternative ways of behaving as abnormal. For example, Sabin (1975) found cultural bias when clinicians used assessment techniques with non-English-speaking patients such as Mexican-Americans. The patient's emotional problems and symptoms were often misunderstood. This may explain why there is a much higher incidence of serious mental illness, such as schizophrenia, diagnosed in ethnic minorities in the UK and the United States (see Study 1.4, page 18).

In physical illness, the cultural differences between a patient and doctor would not contribute to the diagnosis made, because objective measures (such as urine samples or blood tests) are undertaken to confirm the illness.

The medical model and maladaptiveness

The idea that mental disorders affect the way a person functions in the world has been acknowledged in the medical model. The diagnosis of mental illness in America since 1980 has involved assessment of the psychological, social and occupational functioning of the individual in the months prior to the 'illness'. Collecting information about a patient's level of functioning can help the psychiatrist to make a more informed decision about whether treatment is needed.

While this assessment has been widely welcomed, some critics – for example, Davison and Neale (2001) – have argued that it is a further subjective measurement which assumes that there is some form of normal (or average) functioning.

In addition, receiving a psychiatric diagnosis in itself can create negative consequences for the individual. Davison and Neale (2001) point out that, when a person has been diagnosed with a serious mental illness, friends and loved ones often begin to react differently towards them. Employment may be difficult to find. Adaptive functioning can be compromised as a result of the diagnosis (see Study 1.3, page 17).

The medical model and distress

To come to the notice of a psychiatrist, the patient (or their family or friends) must have reported distress. This definition of abnormality is therefore apparent in the medical model. However, Laing (1967) argued that, although people who are considered to be mentally ill are often unpredictable, it is usually other people who are disturbed by their behaviour, rather than the individual sufferers themselves. This raises ethical issues about the individual's right to behave as he or she pleases.

1.5 Diagnosis of abnormal behaviour

Central to the medical model of abnormality is the ability to classify and diagnose mental disorders. The main purpose of a diagnostic system is to enable a suitable programme of treatment to be chosen. Kraeplin (1981 [1896]) was the first to propose a system consisting of two major groups of mental diseases. His idea formed the basis of the more complex *Diagnostic and Statistical Manual of Mental Disorders* (*DSM*) in use today. It is used mainly in the USA but is referred to in UK training programmes for mental health professionals. The manual was first published in 1952 by the American Psychiatric Association (APA). Psychiatrists use the manual when diagnosing mental illness. It contains a description of mental health disorders and their symptoms. The *DSM* has been periodically updated and psychiatrists are currently using the fourth edition (*DSM IV*), which was published in 1994. The earlier versions classified 16 different types of mental disorder (see Figure 1.6). Since the third edition in 1980, factors such as general medical conditions, psychosocial and environmental problems have also been considered, indicating a movement towards combining physical and psychological knowledge and understanding. This is known as the **multi-axial classification system**. The individual is rated on five separate scales (or axes), which broadens the amount of information gathered from the patient during the diagnosis.

On Axis 1 the clinical syndromes are considered (see Figure 1.6), apart from personality disorders, which are considered separately.

On Axis 2 the personality disorders are considered.

The categories have been split in this way to ensure that clinicians do not miss a further problem because they focus solely on the current one. For example, a person may present with a substance abuse problem but also have an antisocial personality disorder.

On Axis 3 the clinician should note any general medical conditions that could affect the patient's mental health. For example, if the patient has cancer this is likely to impact on their psychological well-being. A diagnosis of diabetes might explain why a child has become

Category	Brief description
Delirium, dementia, amnesia and other cognitive disorders	These are the organic mental disorders – known to have a definable physical cause such as brain disease
Schizophrenic and other psychotic disorders	Serious mental disorders where the individual loses touch with reality (see Chapter 3)
Substance-related disorders	Addiction to alcohol, opiates, cocaine, amphetamines or other substances causing serious behavioural problems
Mood disorders	Depressive symptoms or mood swings from excessive highs to extreme lows (see Chapter 3)
Anxiety disorders	Any disorder where the individual feels very anxious, such as phobias and obsessive compulsive disorder (see Chapter 2)
Somatoform disorders	A history of physical complaints without any obvious physical cause – for example, hypochondria
Dissociative disorders	A sudden alteration in consciousness affecting memory and identity – for example, total memory loss (non-organic)
Adjustment disorders	The development of major emotional or behavioural symptoms following a stressful life event
Disorders usually diagnosed in infancy, childhood or adolescence	Intellectual, physical or emotional disorders usually beginning early in life, such as autism and attention deficit disorder
Personality disorders	Inflexible and maladaptive patterns of adult behaviour – there are ten disorders listed, including antisocial personality disorder
Sexual and gender identity disorders	Unconventional sexual gratification, sexual dysfunction and gender identity disorders
Impulse control disorders	The person's behaviour is inappropriate and out of control, for example kleptomania – repeated stealing without any monetary need
Factitious disorders	People who intentionally produce physical illness because of the need to assume a sick role
Sleep disorders	Sleep is disturbed (either too much or too little) or unusual events occur during sleep (such as sleep walking)
Eating disorders	Anorexia nervosa, where the person avoids eating, or bulimia nervosa, where binge eating is followed by purging (see Chapter 2)
Other conditions that may be a focus of clinical attention	Psychological factors that may affect the physical condition of a person such as marital- or work-related difficulties

Figure 1.6: The major categories of mental disorder as identified by *DSM IV*

aggressive, instead of diagnosing a conduct disorder. Treatment given for physical conditions may also affect the way a patient responds to mental health care.

Axes 1–3 are compulsory when making a diagnosis whereas the next two axes are currently optional.

On Axis 4, information about any psychosocial and environmental problems experienced by the patient are considered. For example, problems with housing, access to health care or difficulties within the family.

Axis 5 measures the patient's current level of adaptive functioning. The patient is rated on a scale of 1–100 for social, psychological and occupational well-being. A score of 90 indicates superior functioning over a wide range of activities. The patient is doing well at work, has good social relationships and is coping psychologically. A score of below 10 would indicate that the patient was in danger of severely hurting others, or had made serious suicide attempts and was functioning very poorly.

The inclusion of Axes 4 and 5 reflects movement towards a more interactionist approach to mental health problems. Most psychiatrists now accept that mental health difficulties occur as a result of the interaction between biological, psychological and sociological factors. Previously, diagnosis involved simply classifying a patient in a clinical category – for example, schizophrenia – and prescribing drug treatment. Since 1980 the patient's needs have been assessed more broadly, and they can be referred to other agencies if necessary. For example, if a patient is having difficulty finding a job, there may be work schemes within the community, specialising in helping people with mental health problems (see Chapter 4). If a patient is having difficulty with child care, a family social worker might be contacted for assistance and information. A **multi-disciplinary** approach can now been adopted, where professionals from different areas of health and social care work together.

Each category in *DSM IV* includes a list of symptoms and other information to help diagnosis, such as how many symptoms should be apparent. These are called **operational diagnostic criteria**. For example, the diagnosis of bipolar depression requires the presence of an elevated mood, plus three additional symptoms, during the manic phase. The patient should also have experienced episodes of depression (see Figure 1.7).

Symptoms of the depressive phase	Symptoms of the manic phase
1. Sad, depressed mood	1. Increase in activity at work, socially and sexually
2. Loss of interest and pleasure in usual activities	2. Unusual talkativeness and rapid speech
3. Difficulties in sleeping – disturbance in sleep patterns or sleeping for long periods	3. Less than the usual amount of sleep required
4. Shift in activity level, becoming lethargic (drowsy) or agitated	4. Flight of ideas or subjective impression that thoughts are racing
5. Poor appetite and weight loss, or increased appetite and weight gain	5. Inflated self-esteem, belief one has special powers, talents and abilities
6. Loss of energy, great fatigue	6. Distractibility, attention easily diverted
7. Negative self-concept, self-reproach, self-blame, feelings of guilt and worthlessness	7. Over-involvement in activities with negative consequences, e.g. reckless spending

Figure 1.7: The signs and symptoms of bipolar disorder as listed in *DSM IV*

REFLECTIVE Activity

Choose five symptoms of the depressive phase from Figure 1.7. Consider the impact they might have on the patient's functioning. How would depression affect social, psychological and occupational functioning? Repeat the exercise looking at symptoms of the manic phase. Does this help to explain why people in the manic phase do not believe they are ill?

A second method of classification in use in the UK today is a manual published by the World Health Organization (WHO). It is known as the *International Classification of Diseases, Injuries and Causes of Death* (*ICD*) and contains a comprehensive listing of all diseases. A section on mental health problems was first included in the *ICD* in 1948 and has been periodically updated. This section lists ten major categories of mental disorders and their operational diagnostic criteria. *DSM IV* has 16 categories of mental disorders. The difference occurs because the *ICD* uses a smaller number of general categories. For example, the *ICD* has one category to cover neurotic, stress-related and somatoform disorders, whereas the *DSM* lists these as separate categories. In one instance however (disorders of childhood), the *ICD* has three specific categories, whereas the *DSM* uses a general description (see Figure 1.8). The difference in categories and the more precise way that disorders have been categorised in *DSM IV*, has led to claims that it is more reliable than *ICD*.

Some experts have claimed that systems of classification are needed to help communication about the nature of the patients' problems. It helps mental health professionals decide which treatment to offer and make predictions about recovery. The system also enables research to be undertaken with comparable groups of patients, which can help develop and improve treatment methods.

ICD categories	*DSM* categories
1. Organic, including symptomatic mental disorders	Similar
2. Schizophrenia, schizotypal and delusional disorders	Similar
3. Mental and behavioural disorders due to substance abuse	Similar
4. Mood (affective) disorders	Similar
5. Neurotic, stress-related and somatoform disorders	Split into four categories: anxiety, somatoform, dissociative and adjustment disorders
6. Behavioural and emotional disorders with onset in childhood	6, 7 and 8 in *ICD* are grouped under one category in *DSM*
7. Disorders of psychological development	
8. Mental retardation	
9. Disorders of adult personality and behaviour	Similar
10. Behavioural syndromes – physiological disturbances and physical factors	Split into two categories – sleep and eating disorders – in *DSM*
11. Unspecified mental disorder	Similar

Figure 1.8: The major categories of mental disorder identified in *ICD 10* compared to *DSM IV*

EVALUATIVE COMMENT

Both *DSM* and *ICD* group together symptoms in categories. Psychiatrists look for symptoms and make a decision about whether a person has a mental disorder or not. The classification system therefore has the same limitation as a closed questionnaire. A 'yes' or 'no' decision must be made. Pilgrim (2000) argued that the difference between mental health and mental abnormality is a matter of degree. For example, most people experience depression. The severity of the condition is a more important indicator of mental disorder. A dimensional classification system would measure the patient on a ranked scale rather than simply ticking off the number of symptoms seen. Axes 4 and 5 in the *DSM* do use a dimensional classification system, however these axes are currently optional during diagnosis.

Interestingly, neither system actually uses the term 'mental illness', opting instead to describe 'mental disorders'. Cooper (1994) argued that there is little evidence so far, that many psychiatric diagnoses are caused by physiology. For example, there is still great debate about the causes of 'illnesses' such as schizophrenia or depression (see Chapter 3). The use of the term 'disorder' neatly avoids the need to debate the meaning or value of the medical model.

1.6 Interpersonal issues in assessment

The medical model and the current classification system can be viewed as an objective method of diagnosing mental illness. However, the assessment of mental health takes place between people. Mental health practitioners are affected in their judgements by interpersonal issues such as labelling, stereotyping, and the roles and expectations of both patient and doctor.

Stereotyping and labelling

Scheff (1966) criticised the medical model of mental illness and in particular the diagnosis of schizophrenia. He thought that 'schizophrenia' was a label attached to unusual behaviour. He claimed that people labelled schizophrenic did not break formal and obvious rules, such as stealing or hurting someone. Instead they were involved in residual rule breaking (for example, talking to themselves). This bizarre behaviour made others feel uncomfortable but was relatively inconsequential. Scheff argued that lots of people break residual rules, but only those who are referred to a psychiatrist acquire a label. The label influences the way in which a person will continue to behave.

In hospital, patients with schizophrenia would be encouraged to see themselves as suffering from a condition beyond their control. They would receive attention and sympathy, encouraging them to settle into their new social identity. They may act 'crazy' because this is what is expected of them. The label will also determine the reactions of other people. Scheff thought that it was extremely difficult to remove the mental illness label even if the individual stopped behaving unusually. Once judged 'insane', other people would become motivated to look for behaviour to confirm the label. Scheff (1966) argued that receiving a psychiatric diagnosis thus created a stigma or mark of social disgrace.

Study 1.2

AIM Rosenhan (1973) provided a powerful example of the effect of labelling on mental health patients.

METHOD He asked eight psychologically healthy people to arrange appointments at different hospitals. They were to complain that they could hear a voice in their head, which said words like 'thud' and 'hollow'. All eight pseudo-patients were admitted to hospital; seven were diagnosed with schizophrenia. Rosenhan instructed the participants to act normally once they were in hospital, not to take any medication given and to try to convince staff that they were sane. They were also asked to observe and record their experiences on the ward.

RESULT The pseudo-patients were kept on the ward for an average of 19 days. The longest stay was 52 days. None of the patients managed to convince medical staff that they were sane. The following observations were documented.

1. Normal behaviour was viewed as abnormal by staff. All the pseudo-patients took notes throughout the study. Staff did not ask the participants why they were doing this. Instead, in one instance, a nurse recorded 'patient engages in writing behaviour', implying that it was a bizarre symptom of the disorder. Waiting outside the canteen before lunch was interpreted as 'oral-acquisitive syndrome' by a psychiatrist. Pacing the corridors out of boredom was seen as 'nervousness'.

2. Patients and staff were strictly segregated and normal interaction was discouraged. There was very little contact with doctors, and questions from the pseudo-patients about their treatment or discharge from the hospital were ignored. Psychiatrists rarely even stopped or made eye contact during these interactions; 71 per cent of the time they moved on, with their head averted and only stopped to talk 4 per cent of the time.

3. The pseudo-patients reported a loss of rights and privacy, little constructive activity, and frequent verbal and physical abuse by staff. This led to feelings of powerlessness and a loss of identity, which could again be interpreted as symptoms of their 'illness', rather than a response to the social role they had been given.

4. Other patients did recognise 'normality' and asked the pseudo-patients if they were reporters!

CONCLUSION Mental health patients and staff adopt social roles and labels that affect behaviour, thoughts and feelings. It is extremely difficult for patients to escape the label of their mental illness diagnosis. The label can create a self-fulfilling prophecy, with patients living up to the limited expectations of staff.

EVALUATIVE COMMENT

Psychiatrists and staff would not expect that normal people would attempt to gain admittance to a psychiatric hospital. The situation is ecologically invalid because in real life, this would not happen. Kety (1974) defended the staff in Rosenhan's study, claiming they simply made a diagnosis on the basis of apparent symptoms. He argued that a similar misdiagnosis would occur if someone attempted to fake physical symptoms. For example, if a person drank a quart of blood and arrived at hospital vomiting, nursing staff would quite predictably label and treat the patient for a bleeding peptic ulcer. This is not enough evidence to claim that medical science does not know how to diagnose the condition.

The study does provide evidence that patients are treated differently after diagnosis as a result of being labelled. *DSM IV* explicitly rejects the use of labels such as 'schizophrenic', recognising that psychiatric diagnoses in the past have caused discrimination and stigma. It recommends instead that clinicians should use the term 'an individual with schizophrenia'. In this way the medical model is attempting to address the criticisms of the anti-psychiatry movement. It is interesting to note that the Rosenhan study is called 'On being sane in insane places'.

More recent research with those suffering from mental health difficulties has shown the effect of stereotyping. A stereotype is a widely held assumption about the personalities, attitudes and behaviour of people based on group membership (Hogg and Vaughan, 1995). People suffering from mental health problems are often negatively stereotyped, leading to discrimination against them.

Study 1.3

AIM The research was undertaken by Faulkner and Layzell (2000) to provide evidence of stereotyping experienced by people suffering mental health problems.

METHOD A total of 584 participants completed a questionnaire, designed to collect information about discrimination. They were also asked how they thought discrimination could be reduced.

RESULT A total of 70 per cent of participants had experienced stereotyping and discrimination; 66 per cent said they had not told people about their difficulties because of the stigma attached to mental distress. This has obvious implications for their recovery, increasing the possibility of self-harm and delaying any subsequent treatment.

The respondents also reported stereotyping from their GP (44 per cent) and other health-care professionals (32 per cent). Many people reported that their physical health symptoms had not been taken seriously as a result of their mental health history. For example, one person said 'My present GP diagnoses everything as a mental symptom.'

A total of 30 per cent had experienced discrimination in the workplace. The most serious examples given included dismissal or compulsory redundancy. Others reported they did not disclose details of their mental health history on job applications, because they feared discrimination.

Another main source of discrimination came from within the family (56 per cent) and from friends (52 per cent). Participants thought that this was because of a lack of knowledge and understanding.

CONCLUSION Mental health patients are negatively stereotyped and can experience discrimination as a result of their diagnosis. This discrimination (and the fear of it) adds to the difficulties of people with mental health problems.

EVALUATIVE COMMENT

Labelling does seem to have an impact on those suffering mental health problems. The theory has been useful in raising awareness of the dangers of stereotyping for professionals involved in mental health care. However, Scheff's (1966) argument that schizophrenia is simply a social role, assigned to those who break residual rules, trivialises a very serious and distressing condition. People with mental health difficulties do exist, and need care and treatment.

In Faulkner and Layzell's (2000) study, 91 per cent of participants believed that discrimination could be reduced by challenging stereotyped views of mental illness. In particular, they believed that the media should be encouraged to make more positive and informed representations of mental illness. They recommended campaigns in schools and the workplace to help educate the general public. Accurate information about mental ill-health should also be provided in GP surgeries.

REFLECTIVE Activity

There are many different words (or labels) to describe a person suffering from mental illness – for example 'nutcase'. Make a list of ten words and decide whether each label is positive or negative. Try the same thing to describe a person suffering from cancer. Can you find any evidence of negative stereotyping towards the mentally ill?

Racism

In the UK, black people are more likely than white people to receive a diagnosis of a severe mental illness, such as schizophrenia (Littlewood and Lipsedge, 1989). The increased likelihood of a diagnosis has been explained as a consequence of the stressful geographical and cultural relocation that black people have undertaken as immigrants to a new country. However, Littlewood and Lipsedge (1989) argued that as the majority of immigrants to Britain in recent history have actually been white, the process of immigration alone can not account for the difference. They also examined the rates of serious mental illness. They were higher, on average, for British-born black people rather than their migrant parents or recent immigrants.

Attempts have also been made to explain the difference by claiming black people are genetically more likely to suffer from mental illness. However, in 1979 the World Health Organization (WHO) conducted a study of the rates of schizophrenia in Europe, North America, Asia and Africa. There was very little difference in the rates of severe mental illness reported across the world. For the genetic argument to hold, higher rates should have been seen in countries with largely black populations.

People from ethnic minorities in Britain often experience a range of disadvantages in the areas of housing, education, health and employment. They can also be subjected to overt racism and prejudice on a daily basis. Littlewood (1980) suggested that what is judged as 'insane' behaviour by some mental health practitioners, may actually be a legitimate and understandable response to disadvantage and racism.

The psychiatric community has also treated black people differently to white people. Hospitalised black people are two to three times more likely to be involuntary patients under the Mental Health Act. Littlewood and Cross (1980) found that black people received higher doses of drugs and are more frequently given electro convulsive therapy (ECT) compared to white patients with the same diagnosis.

Study 1.4

AIM Lewis *et al.* (1990) wanted to investigate the effect of race on psychiatric diagnosis.

METHOD A total of 139 psychiatrists were shown an individual written case history. They were asked to make a judgement on the treatment the patient should have. They were also required to predict whether criminal proceedings should be instigated as a result of the behaviour described. Some psychiatrists were told that the patient was a black African-Caribbean and others that the patient was white. The symptoms described in both case studies were exactly the same.

RESULT Psychiatrists who read the African-Caribbean case study were more likely to recommend drug treatment. The behaviour of their patient was also seen as more violent and criminal.

CONCLUSION Mental health professionals are affected in their judgements by social stereotypes.

EVALUATIVE COMMENT

While the results of this study are quite startling, the psychiatrists were making judgements on a hypothetical case rather than a real patient. A more ecologically valid study might produce different results.

The multi-axial classification system has been widely welcomed by psychiatrists and other mental health professionals. The patient's physical health and preceding life stresses are now taken into consideration, enabling the effect of racism and discrimination to be acknowledged during diagnosis.

Sexism

Sex differences in mental health problems have been documented since the 1970s. Women are more likely than men to be admitted to hospital for treatment with depression in the UK. Walker (1994) reported that in all studies of depression, women (particularly older women) outnumber men by between two to six times. However, there is no sex difference for treatment or diagnosis of severe mental illnesses, such as schizophrenia or bipolar disorder (see Chapter 3).

The medical model of mental illness has traditionally looked to biological reasons to explain why women become more depressed. Changes in the hormone levels associated with the menstrual cycle, childbirth and the menopause have all been identified as possible causes of depression in women. However, Weissman and Klerman (1977) found that whilst there is some evidence of hormonal contribution, it can not account for the large differences. They argued that women are led to believe that their bodies are problematic. For example, women are encouraged by doctors to view the menopause as a difficult time. This becomes a **self-fulfilling**

The effect of hormones on a woman's mood

prophecy, a term used by Rosenthal and Jacobson (1968) to describe the tendency to live up to the expectations of others. Ussher (1989) reported that only 10 per cent of women express any feelings of regret about menopause. However, the 'myth' of a depressed, middle-aged, menopausal woman still persists.

Cochrane (1995) observed that the appearance of sex differences in mental illness is quite recent. Earlier in the twentieth century, men were more likely to be admitted to hospitals than women. Substantially higher rates have only been seen for women since the Second World War. Cochrane argued that it is difficult to see how a major biological difference has become apparent only recently. Other, more social, factors must be at work.

Study 1.5

AIM Brown and Harris (1978) wanted to investigate the social factors that might contribute to depression in women of child-bearing age.

METHOD They interviewed 400 women living in Camberwell, London, between 1969 and 1974 about their psychological health and the quality of their daily life.

RESULT A total of 15 per cent of the women interviewed were depressed and 18 per cent were identified as being on the borderline of depression. Brown and Harris identified the following contributory social factors:

- not having paid employment outside the home

- having 3 or more children under the age of 14 living at home

- not having a close and confiding relationship with a partner

- loss of their own mother in childhood.

Brown and Harris also found that working-class women were five times more likely to be depressed than middle-class women.

CONCLUSION Social factors, such as isolation, poverty and lack of support with child care, contribute to the onset of depression in younger women.

Mental health practitioners can also respond differently to men and women.

Study 1.6

AIM Broverman *et al.* (1970) wanted to investigate the effect of sex role stereotyping on mental health professionals' views of psychological health.

METHOD A group of mental health professionals were asked to define the characteristics of a mentally healthy man, woman or adult.

RESULT The characteristics of a mentally healthy adult corresponded very closely to the description of the healthy man. Women were characterised very differently from a mentally healthy adult. Broverman found that healthy women were supposed to be more submissive, emotional, easily influenced, excitable in a minor crisis and overly concerned about their appearance. They were seen to be less aggressive and unadventurous. Broverman concluded that the description of women by clinicians seemed to be 'an unusual way of describing any mature, healthy individual.'

CONCLUSION Mental health practitioners' definitions of normality appear to be sex-role stereotyped.

EVALUATIVE COMMENT

The Broverman study has not been successfully replicated and may now be outdated. Phillips (1985) found that mental health professionals rated feminine traits favourably in a similar study, although this does not confirm what actually happens in real life. Over the past 30 years there have been changes in the roles of men and women in society.

There are gender, class and racial differences in depression. The incidence of psychological difficulty may be more to do with a lack of power and limited access to resources in society. For example, Cochrane *et al.* (1980) found high rates of depression among unemployed men.

Recent research by MIND has documented that the male suicide rate is almost three times as high as the female rate. Particular concern is being raised about the incidence of suicide in young men. It is possible that men are experiencing similar rates of depression to women but are choosing other means of expressing their psychological distress.

PRACTICAL Activity

Cochrane (1987) argued that the distance to be travelled between stereotypically normal behaviour and the symptoms of depression is shorter for women than for men. List some stereotypically female characteristics and look back to the symptoms of a depressive phase listed in Figure 1.7. Do you agree with Cochrane?

Sick role and expert role

Parsons (1951) was a sociologist who was interested in the way roles are assigned to people. He thought that illness involved accepting a sick role. This is a set of expectations and corresponding sanctions governing the behaviour of the individual. For example, if you have a bad cold during winter, you should stay in bed (the expectation). Going out without a coat would be frowned upon (the sanction). Parsons believed there were four aspects to the sick role.

1. The individual is free from normal social role responsibilities. For example, you can stay away from college for a few days.

2. The individual is not expected to recover by an act of will. The patient must be cared for. In other words, you are not expected to 'pull yourself together'.

3. The state of being ill is undesirable and the sick role therefore includes an obligation to get well. For example, you must recover in time for your exam!

4. Recovery requires seeking out the assistance of technically competent help. For example, your mum goes to the chemist for a cold cure.

The idea of the sick role has been applied to people suffering from mental ill-health. In the medical model, the responsibility for recovery is taken away from the patient. A technically competent expert – the psychiatrist – will prescribe the appropriate treatment. Martin (1999) described a way of helping mental health patients accept the sick role by showing patients pictures of their own brain scans. This process allows the patients to see that their experiences are biological and beyond their control. There is some evidence, however, that other people do not attribute the sick role to those suffering from mental illness.

Study 1.7

AIM Bromley (2002) wanted to investigate the acceptance of the sick role by visitors of mental health patients, compared to patients with physical conditions.

METHOD She compared cards and gifts received by 40 psychiatric patients aged 18 to 65, with those of a matched group of patients who had physical conditions such as asthma, and liver and gastrointestinal disorders.

RESULT The psychiatric patients received almost half as many cards as the medical patients even though they stayed in hospital on average five times longer. The psychiatric patients received just one bunch of flowers throughout the study. On the medical wards, Bromley reported 'you can't move for flowers'.

CONCLUSION Bromley believed that the cards and flowers indicated a validation of the sick role for medical patients. Mental health patients are less likely to be perceived in this way. As one patient commented, 'There's the feeling that mental illness can't be cured, so it's not appropriate to send a "Get Well" card.'

EVALUATIVE COMMENT

There are specific difficulties in applying the sick role to mental health problems. In some disorders, such as anorexia, the individual may refuse to accept that they are ill. Treatment of mental health patients is therefore sometimes given without their consent. This type of intervention is not considered in Parson's model of the sick role.

Critics of the medical model have argued that patients should not be encouraged to avoid responsibility. By adopting a sick role, the individual becomes passively dependent on others. Some researchers – for example, Korchin (1976) – have argued that failure to take control can interfere directly with the recovery process and result in chronic (long-lasting) conditions. Psychological treatments, such as cognitive or behavioural therapy, all require active participation by the client for recovery to begin (see Chapter 4).

The sick role also implies a restoration of health, after treatment has been given. Ralph and Kidder (2000) argued that complete recovery from mental illness is sometimes unobtainable. It is more useful to consider 'recovering' as an ongoing process. They give a useful example, taken from the experience of bereavement, to illustrate their point. Parents whose child has died might

A typical get-well card

never really 'recover' from this, in the sense that nothing feels the same since the loss occurred. However, these parents often experience a process in which the loss is integrated into their lives, so that they are able to continue. Ralph and Kidder called this 'recovering', and they liken the process to the way many people with mental health problems live with and adjust to their problems.

The sick role automatically also creates an expert role. The patient should consult a technically competent person for the appropriate treatment. In the case of the medical model of mental illness this could be a GP, a psychiatrist or a psychiatric nurse. With a more psychogenic approach, the expert would be a clinical psychologist or a counsellor.

Study 1.8

AIM Temerlin (1970) wanted to investigate the impact of a respected authority figure on psychiatric diagnosis.

METHOD Participants listened to a taped interview of a person describing their own life. Psychiatrists, clinical psychologists and psychology students heard the person talk about his happy marriage, good relationships with others and his enjoyment of work. A respected expert in psychiatry then told the participants, either that the man was psychologically healthy or that although he seemed neurotic, he was in fact psychotic. Participants were then asked to judge the person's mental health.

RESULT The participants were affected by the opinion of the expert. Those who were told he was healthy gave a 'normal' diagnosis. Those who were told he was psychotic agreed with this diagnosis.

CONCLUSION Someone with authority and expertise can have a strong influence on the way people are perceived.

EVALUATIVE COMMENT

Again, with Temerlin's study, the participants were making a judgement on a hypothetical case. They may have responded differently if the person was actually in their consulting room. It is difficult to gather information about the real-life roles and interactions between psychiatrists and patients because of ethical considerations.

There are a lot of different 'experts' with differing opinions on the causes and appropriate treatments for mental health problems. This might lead critics to question whether any experts actually exist!

Steinberg (1989) proposed a different way of viewing the roles of patient and practitioner. He believed that:

- **the clinicians are experts in their own speciality**

- **the patients are experts on themselves**

- **the clinicians have a responsibility to teach and to learn.**

Psychiatrists can help the patient to understand the disorder and how the treatment will work. However, doctors and psychiatrists should also be prepared to learn more about their patients. For example, how do they understand the disorder and what do they need?

Demand characteristics of the consultation process

The meeting between a mental health practitioner and their patient is called the consultation process. It is an interpersonal exchange of information that could be subject to 'demand characteristics'. This is where participants in an interaction try to work out what is expected of them and change their behaviour as a result. Demand characteristics often prompt an individual to behave in a way that is predictable, given the circumstances. Psychiatrists are expected to recognise symptoms and make a diagnosis during the consultation process. Patients are expected to display symptoms of mental ill-health.

Their own doctor often refers patients for psychiatric assessment. The doctor will forward relevant information to the psychiatrist before the consultation occurs. This means that the psychiatrist will have some prior knowledge (and possibly expectations) about the patient before they actually meet. Rosenhan (1973) gave a powerful demonstration of the effect of expectation and labelling in his first study (see Study 1.2, page 15). In a follow-up study, he told staff in a psychiatric hospital about his previous findings and asked if they would like to participate in some more research.

Study 1.9

AIM Rosenhan (1973) wanted to show that expectation can alter the type of diagnostic decision made.

METHOD He advised members of a teaching hospital that over a three-month period, some pseudo-patients were going to try to gain a psychiatric diagnosis and admission to the wards. They should therefore expect to see normal people during their consultations and should make a note of any patients they believed were participants in the study. No pseudo-patients were sent.

RESULT During the experimental period, 193 genuine patients were admitted; 41 were confidently identified as pseudo-patients by at least one member of staff.

CONCLUSION Diagnosis of mental illness can be affected by demand characteristics. If practitioners are told to look for normal behaviour, they are more likely to see normal behaviour.

EVALUATIVE COMMENT

Although Rosenhan did gain consent in this second study, there are still ethical problems because deception was used. Also, as the study took place in one hospital, it isn't possible to generalise from the results.

Patients will also have some prior expectations about what will happen during consultation and how they should behave. For example, Davison and Neale (2001) argued that Freud's patients were aware of his theory about the psychosexual stages and the importance of childhood in the development of personality. This caused them to focus on childhood events and sexuality during psychoanalysis. In effect, they told Freud what he wanted to hear. Other important and more current events were possibly overlooked, as both the patient and the practitioner did not feel they were relevant. The same demand characteristics could operate in the medical model, with patients overemphasising physical factors.

The class, race, gender, culture and age of either the patient or the practitioner will also have an impact on the consultation process. For example, Levine and Padilla (1980) found that Hispanic patients disclose less about their problems to non-Hispanic white clinicians than do white patients.

EVALUATIVE COMMENT

The demand characteristics of the consultation process are apparent in physical illnesses as well as in mental health problems. Both doctors and patients are human beings! This does not mean that people should not consult a doctor when they are experiencing physical or mental health problems.

The impact of interpersonal issues such as demand characteristics and stereotyping should be considered when evaluating the medical model. However, it is important not to lose sight of the valuable role psychiatrists and doctors play in alleviating the symptoms of mental disorder.

REFLECTIVE Activity

Summarise three advantages and disadvantages of the medical model. In your opinion do the advantages outweigh the disadvantages? Look back to the first Reflective Activity in this chapter. Have your ideas of 'normal' and 'abnormal' behaviour changed?

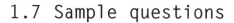

1.7 Sample questions

SAMPLE QUESTION

(a) Name and outline one classification system used in the diagnosis of abnormal behaviour.
(AO1 = 3)   (3 marks)

(b) Outline and briefly discuss one historical approach to abnormality.
(AO1 = 2, AO2 = 3)   (5 marks)

(c) Discuss at least two interpersonal issues in clinical assessment.
(AO1 = 5, AO2 = 7)   (12 marks)

Total AO1 marks = 10 Total AO2 marks = 10 Total = 20 marks

QUESTIONS, ANSWERS AND COMMENTS

(a) Figure 1.11 names and describes some of the criteria used to define abnormality. Complete the table by giving a short description of criteria (i) and (iv) that are named in the table, and naming the criteria described in (ii) and (iii) below.
(AO1 = 4)   (4 marks)

Criterion	Description
Deviation from statistical norms	(i)
(ii)	Defines abnormality as a breaking of society's standards
(iii)	Behaviour is abnormal if it causes harm to the individual or to society
Personal distress	(iv)

Figure 1.11: Some of the criteria used to define abnormality

(b) Suggest one reason why statistical norms and personal distress are not each on their own sufficient to define abnormality.
(AO2 = 4)   (4 marks)

(c) Describe and discuss the medical model of abnormality.
(AO1 = 6, AO2 = 6)   (12 marks)

Total AO1 marks = 10 Total AO2 marks = 10 Total = 20 marks

Answer to (a)

(i) Abnormality is behaviour that is statistically infrequent.

(ii) Deviation from social norms.

(iii) Maladaptiveness.

(iv) Abnormality causes distress to others.

Comment: 3 marks awarded. No mark given for (iv) because personal distress causes unhappiness in the individual and not others.

Answer to (b)

Deviation from statistical norm is not sufficient because people whose behaviour is uncommon but desirable would be defined as abnormal. For example, someone with musical ability is statistically infrequent but not antisocial. Personal distress is when a person is upset and goes to see a doctor to get some help.

Comment: 3 marks awarded. 1 mark given for a brief description of personal distress but no limitation has been given.

Answer to (c)

The medical model assumes mental disorders are caused by biological factors such as genetics or brain chemistry. Even though a physical cause has not been found for all mental disorders, the medical model assumes it's only a matter of time before a scientific explanation is found. Psychiatrists use a diagnostic manual in hospitals to decide if a patient is mentally ill. It groups together symptoms seen in each type of disorder. If someone has the right number of symptoms they will be diagnosed. The doctor can then offer treatments, such as antidepressant drugs.

The medical model says the patient is not responsible for their illness. This is good because the patient and their family may feel reassured that it's not their fault. Also trained doctors and nurses will look after the patient.

A problem with the medical model is that it labels people and this might create prejudice and discrimination. Rosenhan found that once someone was given the label of schizophrenia they could not escape it. Eight normal people were admitted to hospital complaining of hearing voices. On the ward they acted normally but psychiatrists treated them as if they were mad. They were ignored and everything they did was seen as a symptom. Szasz agreed that the label of mental illness creates a self-fulfilling prophecy. People are treated as if they are ill so they start acting that way.

Psychologists would argue that social and environmental factors cause mental health disorders, and not biology. They think that people should be treated as individuals and not as groups of symptoms.

Comment: 9 marks awarded (5 for AO1 and 4 for AO2). Although this is a short answer the description is relevant and accurate. The discussion includes a balance of strengths and weaknesses although some of the points made are rather brief.

Overall (parts a, b and c) the answer is well-organised, but could be improved by adding further information. A good answer.

1.8 FURTHER READING

Introductory texts

Davison, G.C. & Neale, J.M. 2001: **Abnormal Psychology**. 8th edition, Wiley, New York

Gross, R. 2001: **Psychology: The Science of Mind and Behaviour**. Hodder & Stoughton, London

Jarvis, M., Putwain, D. & Dwyer, D. 2002: **Angles on Atypical Psychology**. Nelson Thornes, Cheltenham

Stirling, J.D. & Hellewell, S.E. 1999: **Psychopathology, Atypical Development and Abnormal Behaviour**. Routledge, London and New York

Specialist sources

Cochrane, R. 1987: **The Social Creation of Mental Illness**. Longman, London

Littlewood, R. & Lipsedge, M. 1997: **Aliens and Alienists: Ethnic Minorities and Psychiatry**. 3rd Ed. Routledge, London

Szasz, T. 1962: **The Myth of Mental Illness**. Harper & Row, New York

Ussher, J. 1991: **Women's Madness. Misogyny or Mental Illness?** Harvester Wheatsheaf

Useful websites

www.mind.org.uk Useful information on mental health

www.news.bbc.co.uk Go to health/medical notes for up-to-date articles on all aspects of mental health

www.sane.org.uk Useful information on mental health

2
Anxiety and eating disorders

2.1 Introduction

Everyone has experienced fear – for example, if you are faced with a stressful event like an important examination you are likely to feel worried and stressed. Psychologists believe that being frightened can have a protective function, because it prepares an individual to take action when threatened. Increasing worry about upcoming exams may be the thing that motivates you to begin revising! Fear also acts as an alarm system to warn individuals of potential danger. However, some people feel afraid without any obvious external trigger, or respond fearfully to harmless stimuli. For example, arachnophobia is an excessive fear of spiders. This type of emotional response is known as anxiety and it can disrupt normal, everyday functioning. Anxiety disorders are sometimes so severe that the individual requires the help of a mental health practitioner.

There are four main anxiety disorders listed in the *DSM IV* and *ICD 10* manuals used by doctors and psychiatrists (see Chapter 1). These are generalised anxiety, phobias, obsessive compulsive behaviours, and post-traumatic stress. Anxiety is a central symptom of them all. They are categorised in *DSM IV* and *ICD 10* as **neuroses**. Individual sufferers are clearly aware that their anxiety is unusual; they don't lose touch with reality. However, the course of the illness, and the situations in which the individual becomes anxious, differ in each type of disorder.

2.2 Symptoms of anxiety

Anxiety affects an individual psychologically and physically. It can range from mild to extreme (panic) attacks.

Psychological symptoms – A person suffering from anxiety will have feelings of unease, panic and dread. He or she may feel that, with very high levels of anxiety, they are about to die or lose control of their bodily functions. Patients may find it difficult to concentrate, and feel 'jumpy' or unable to relax.

Physical (or somatic) symptoms – Physical symptoms include an increased heart rate, known as **palpitations**, and an increase in the rate of breathing. This is called **hyperventilation**, and is experienced as extreme breathlessness and a sensation of tightness in the chest. Hyperventilation leads to a reduction of carbon monoxide in the blood, which causes the person to feel faint. He or she may also have a dry mouth, a tingling sensation in the hands or feet, headache, back pain and a frequent urge to go to the toilet. Some people actually shake with fear.

REFLECTIVE Activity

Look at the physical symptoms of anxiety. How do they contribute to the psychological symptoms experienced?

Generalised anxiety disorder (GAD)

Generalised anxiety occurs in a continuous and unfocused way. There are no specific or obvious external triggers to create a feeling of anxiety. In effect the person is anxious about anything and everything. It is sometimes called free-floating anxiety. It typically begins in the person's mid-teens (Barlow, 1986) and affects about 5 per cent of the population. GAD can have a highly disruptive effect on everyday life and is one of the more difficult anxiety disorders to treat successfully.

Phobias

A patient with a phobia has an irrational and disproportionate fear of particular objects, activities or situations. A phobic person can often acknowledge that their response to the phobic stimulus (such as a spider) is out of proportion to the actual danger it can cause. However, he or she will respond with extreme anxiety if faced with the stimulus, and is highly motivated to avoid any possible contact with it. *DSM IV* identifies three categories of phobia: agoraphobia, social phobia and specific phobias.

AGORAPHOBIA

This term literally means 'a fear of market-places'. An agoraphobic person will have a fear of open spaces. The disorder usually involves **panic attacks**, which are very distressing episodes of extreme anxiety often involving palpitations and hyperventilation. People experiencing panic attacks can think they are having a heart attack because the symptoms are quite similar. Usually the person feels most vulnerable to panic attacks when they are furthest away from home or the help of someone they trust. Consequently they will also avoid closed public spaces (like a supermarket), travelling on public transport or being in crowds. Severely agoraphobic people avoid going out altogether and become virtual 'prisoners' in their own homes. Agoraphobia accounts for 10–50 per cent of all phobias referred for treatment (Gross and McIlveen, 2000). The condition can last for many years.

SOCIAL PHOBIA

People with social phobia have fears about social situations and interactions, such as meeting new people or eating in public. It is also characterised by a fear of embarrassment or humiliation. The most stressful situations are those where the individual would be under the scrutiny of others.

Social phobia usually begins in adolescence or early adulthood (Stirling and Hellewell, 1999) and can last for years. In contrast to the other phobias, males are affected as often as females. Sufferers sometimes try to get over their difficulties with alcohol or other drugs, so drug dependency can be another potential problem.

Someone with social phobia would not be happy in this situation

SPECIFIC PHOBIA

Specific phobias involve excessive anxiety with regard to specific objects or situations. There are five major sub-types listed in *DSM IV*:

1. animal type – for example, snakes or spiders

2. the natural environment type – for example, fear of heights or thunder storms

3. blood, injection, illness or injury type – for example, fear of cancer or death

4. situational type – for example, fear of flying or getting in a lift

5. other type – this covers specific phobias that do not fit into the other categories (for example, a fear of vacuum cleaners).

Illness or injury type phobias tend to occur in middle age. Other specific phobias usually develop in childhood, but can occur at any time. Women are much more commonly affected than men (Stirling and Hellewell, 1999). It is the most common type of phobia and the least disruptive to everyday life, as the individual can often simply avoid the specific feared stimulus.

PRACTICAL Activity

Test your knowledge of specific phobias by trying the quiz shown in Figure 2.2. Answers are given at the end of the chapter.

---

1. Aquaphobia is fear of: (a) the colour blue (b) examinations (c) water (d) scuba diving

2. Mysophobia is the fear of: (a) yourself (b) rats (c) cancer (d) germs

3. Siderophobia is the fear of: (a) cider (b) lying down (c) railways (d) men called Sid

4. Acrophobia is the fear of: (a) acrobats (b) high places (c) corpses (d) being underground

5. Zoophobia is the fear of: (a) the zoo (b) cages (c) animals (d) safari parks

6. Pathophobia is the fear of: (a) pavements (b) losing your mind (c) strangers (d) disease

7. Astraphobia is the fear of: (a) thunder and lightening (b) stars (c) bright lights (d) astronauts

8. Belonophobia is the fear of: (a) balloons (b) buttons (c) quiz games (d) needles

9. Algophobia is the fear of: (a) pain (b) false teeth (c) injections (d) playing cards

10. Triskaidekaphobia is the fear of (a) trees (b) number 13 (c) horoscopes (d) threesomes

---

Figure 2.2: Phobias quiz

Obsessive compulsive disorder (OCD)

This condition is characterised by obsessional thoughts followed by compulsive **rituals**. Unpleasant thoughts, which may feel beyond the person's control, create feelings of anxiety. To reduce the distress, he or she will engage in repetitive behaviour, known as rituals. For example, a person begins to have persistent worrying thoughts about contamination by germs. To reduce the anxiety, the person begins to wash. Anxiety levels drop. When he or she stops washing, the thoughts return and the person has to perform the ritual again.

OCD sufferers recognise that their behaviour is unusual and senseless, but they can not stop. If the compulsive behaviour is interrupted (or prevented), the sufferer can experience extreme distress, which reduces only when the ritual is successfully carried out. OCD can therefore be severely disruptive to everyday life.

Obsessive compulsive disorder typically begins in early adulthood (Stirling and Hellewell, 1999). Once established it can persist for many years. The number of people seeking help for OCD has increased dramatically in the last ten years. It is now thought to affect up to 3 per cent of the population at some time in their life.

REFLECTIVE Activity

Performing rituals is also part of everyday behaviour. For example, some students always take a lucky mascot into exams with them. Can you think of five examples of ritual behaviour in everyday life? What separates these rituals from the symptoms of OCD?

Post-traumatic stress disorder (PTSD)

People often develop symptoms of anxiety after experiencing a very distressing event (a trauma). Usually the reaction lasts for a few weeks and then fades away. In some people, the symptoms continue or re-emerge after a substantial delay. This is known as post-traumatic stress disorder. The symptoms are divided into three clusters:

1. persistent symptoms of anxiety

2. avoidance behaviour (for example, refusing to drive again after a bad car accident)

3. involuntary re-experiencing of the event through intrusive, persistent memories and disturbed dreams.

Green (1994) reports that PTSD develops in about 25 per cent of people who experience potentially traumatic events, ranging from 12 per cent for accidents to 80 per cent for rape. The likelihood of PTSD developing increases with the severity of the event, but obviously there are individual differences in how people respond to trauma. Breslau *et al.* (1998) found that given exposure to trauma, women are twice as likely as men to develop PTSD. The recovery environment (such as support groups) can also have an effect. If a person has a good support network after experiencing a trauma, he or she is less likely to be affected by PTSD.

2.3 Explanations and therapies for anxiety disorders

Biological approach

BIOCHEMISTRY

Anxiety disorders have been linked with disturbances in the brain's **neurotransmitter** systems.

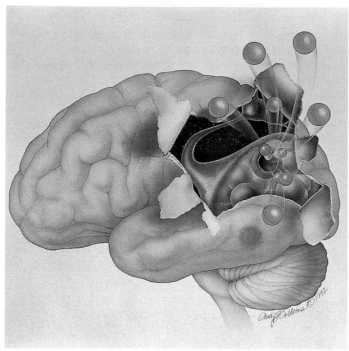

Figure 2.3: Neurotransmitters are implicated in anxiety

The brain produces chemicals to pass messages between neurons in the nervous system. These substances are known as neurotransmitters. Scientists have considered the possible role of the neurotransmitter gamma-aminobutyric acid (GABA).

When you are faced with a frightening event (such as a car accident) neurons throughout the brain fire and create the experience of anxiety. In normal anxiety, the neural firing sets off the production of GABA to slow down neural activity. This ensures that the anxiety subsides. Someone with an anxiety disorder may have a defect in his or her GABA system, which means anxiety is not brought under control. Anxiety disorders may result from too little GABA in the brain.

Reflective Activity

Look back at the descriptions of the four main anxiety disorders. Can they all be explained by the biochemical approach? Which (if any) seem to indicate more social or environmental causes?

EVALUATIVE COMMENT

Brain chemistry may provide a possible explanation for some anxiety disorders, such as general anxiety disorder (GAD). Others, like specific type phobia are less convincingly explained by this approach. In specific phobias, one particular stimulus alone provokes an unusual anxiety response. The rest of the time, the individual responds normally to stressful situations.

BIOLOGICAL TREATMENTS

Sedatives or tranquillisers have been developed to reduce anxiety. They are known as anxiolytic drugs and are among the most widely prescribed drugs (SANE, 2002). Barbiturates were the first major category of drugs used to treat anxiety. Because they were life threatening if someone took an overdose, they have been largely replaced by benzodiazipines. This group of anxiolytic drugs is known to affect GABA neurotransmitters in the brain. They reduce anxiety by enhancing the release of GABA.

More recently, drugs that were originally developed to treat depression have become popular in treating anxiety disorders, in particular OCD and social phobia. Antidepressants such as Prozac (see Chapter 3) are prescribed. This highlights that depression may be an important component of an anxiety disorder.

EVALUATIVE COMMENT

A major problem with anxiolytic drugs is that they are addictive. Patients can develop dependency, making withdrawal symptoms likely (Herbert, 1995).

Also the anxiety disorder can return if the patient stops taking medication. This is because biological treatments control the symptoms of anxiety but do not address the cause. Other more psychological approaches to anxiety, such as cognitive or psychodynamic psychotherapy, attempt to alleviate symptoms and understand where the anxiety comes from.

Genetics

There is some evidence of a genetic vulnerability to developing anxiety disorders.

Study 2.1

AIM Slater and Shields (1969) investigated the role of heredity in anxiety disorders.

METHOD They examined 17 pairs of identical (monozygotic, or MZ) twins and 28 non-identical (dizygotic, or DZ) twins, where one twin had been diagnosed with an anxiety disorder. Slater and Shields wanted to know if the other (or co-twin) also had an anxiety disorder. As identical twins share 100 per cent of their genes, it was expected that they would have very similar psychological functioning. This similarity is called a **concordance rate**. A lower concordance rate was expected for DZ twins because they only share 50 per cent of their genes.

RESULT A total of 49 per cent of the MZ co-twins were also diagnosed as having an anxiety disorder. In the DZ twins, as expected, the concordance rate was lower, at 4 per cent.

CONCLUSION The study provides some evidence for the role of genetics in the development of anxiety disorders.

EVALUATIVE COMMENT

Evolutionary psychologists like Hugdahl and Ohman (Hugdahl *et al.*, 1977) argue that some phobias (such as a fear of snakes) do have a genetic component. They believe people react negatively to certain animals because they were sources of danger in our evolutionary past. However, while Slater and Shields' study does provide evidence that genetic factors are implicated in anxiety, if it were a wholly genetic disorder the concordance rate for MZ twins should be 100 per cent and for DZ twins 50 per cent. Other factors must be involved to make the affected twin more vulnerable or protect the non-affected twin. Also, the sample size was very small and not representative of the population as a whole.

Finally, while research into the role of genetics is ongoing, the approach does not as yet provide a method of treatment.

Psychodynamic approach

Freud (1909) believed there are two types of anxiety. **Objective anxiety** (or realistic anxiety) is caused by an external event. It can often be dealt with in a rational way. For example, worry about a driving test can be overcome by booking more driving lessons. With this type of anxiety there is an environmental cause and it is reasonable to feel anxious.

Neurotic anxiety is caused by internal psychological (or intrapsychic) conflict. It is the result of the early power struggles between parent and child as the child's personality forms. Freud thought that personality developed in stages and consisted of three parts (see Chapter 1 in *Introducing Psychology*). The id (which you are born with) is an unconscious part of the personality and is composed of sexual and aggressive instincts. The ego develops in early childhood to keep these basic instincts in check. Freud thought that during this time, parents punish the young child whenever it fails to control sexual or aggressive desires. The child's wishes are often in conflict with adult expectations, creating tension and distress. To reduce the conflict these painful encounters with adults are repressed (kept from conscious awareness). In adulthood, neurotic anxiety occurs when a person is faced with a situation that unconsciously reminds them of this repressed conflict. It represents the fear of the consequences of expressing the id-driven impulses.

Neurotic anxiety is dealt with through an unconscious distortion of reality by means of 'defence mechanisms'. These allow the ego to discharge some id energy (sexual or aggressive) without facing up to its true nature. In effect, defence mechanisms are a disguised outlet for basic desires. Examples of some defence mechanisms can be seen in Figure 2.4.

Name of defence	Description	Example of anxiety disorder
Repression	Pushing an unhappy memory into the unconscious	A person with a social phobia was made to perform in front of an audience as a child; they have no memory of this event
Displacement	Transferring negative feelings on to an innocent target	A person with a fear of snakes may actually want to strangle someone!
Denial	Refusing to acknowledge something because it is painful	A person with a phobia may go to great lengths to avoid what they fear and deny they are doing so
Reaction formation	Consciously feeling the exact opposite of what you unconsciously feel	A person with OCD who fears dirt and compulsively washes may really want to soil his or her self

Figure 2.4: Some examples of defence mechanisms and anxiety disorders

PRACTICAL Activity

Using Figure 2.4 try to explain the following anxiety disorders from a psychodynamic perspective:

1. a person with social phobia who thinks everyone hates them

2. a person with an illness phobia who is terribly afraid of dying

3. a person with an obsessive compulsive disorder who claims they had a very happy childhood

4. a person who has developed post-traumatic stress disorder after a very minor accident where no one was hurt.

Ask another student of psychology to do the same exercise. Compare your results. Does this activity help you to evaluate the psychodynamic approach?

EVALUATIVE COMMENT

This approach is very subjective, as perhaps you have discovered. It is possible to interpret the same symptoms in different ways.

Critics of Freudian theory argue that it is culturally specific. At the time Freud was practising (during the reign of Queen Victoria), expression of sexual desire was seen as distasteful. Freud developed his theories in a culture of repression. Today, however, sexual desires are much more openly acknowledged. In spite of increased liberalism, there had been no significant reduction in people with anxiety disorders. This implies that anxiety is not solely caused by repressed sexual instincts.

PSYCHODYNAMIC TREATMENT

Freud was one of the first practitioners to develop and use **psychotherapy**. Psychotherapy is a social interaction in which a trained professional tries to help another person feel differently. There are now many different types of psychotherapy. The psychodynamic approach assumes that the patient (or client) does not understand what motivates them. The therapy aims to help people gain insight into why they behave, feel and think the way they do. The therapist analyses what the patient says, to uncover the hidden, unconscious cause of neurotic anxiety.

Clients are encouraged to talk about whatever comes into their mind without interruption. This is known as **free association**. During free association, the client's ego will try to protect itself from any threat of the id emerging, using defence mechanisms (see Figure 2.4). The therapist analyses the latent (hidden) meaning of these defences to help the client gain insight. The client's dreams are also examined for evidence of symbolic representations of repressed childhood conflict. These interpretations are explained to the client, to help them make sense of the true cause of their distress. Freud believed insight helped clients to gain greater control of their emotions and reduced neurotic anxiety. You may remember the next study from your AS studies (see Chapter 4 in *Introducing Psychology*).

Sexual and aggressive instincts have become central themes in entertainment since Freud practised

Study 2.2

AIM Freud wanted to help a friend's young son (Little Hans) to recover from a phobia of horses.

METHOD Freud asked the child's father to send him details of the phobia by letter to enable him to uncover the underlying cause. The father told Freud that Little Hans was afraid of large white horses with black blinkers and black around the mouth. He had become terrified to leave the house and was very anxious that a horse might bite him or would fall down. Freud made an analysis of this information.

RESULT Freud interpreted the phobia as the conscious representation of the Oedipus complex. At around five years of age, Freud believed that a male child desired his mother in a sexual way and perceived his father as a rival. The boy feared that the father would discover his desires and castrate him. Consequently, the boy unconsciously wanted his father to die. For Little Hans, the white horse symbolised his father, who wore glasses (the horse had blinkers) and had a moustache (the horse was black around the mouth). Fear of being bitten by the horse represented castration anxiety, whilst fear of a horse falling down was his unconscious wish to see his father dead.

CONCLUSION Phobias are caused by neurotic anxiety and are linked to repressed childhood experiences.

EVALUATIVE COMMENT

Supporting evidence for Freudian theory is restricted to reports of case studies undertaken with a small sample of patients. In the case of Little Hans, Freud only met his patient once and relied mainly on correspondence from the boy's father. As Little Hans had witnessed a horse collapse and die in the street, the phobia could have been a learned response, rather than an unconscious Oedipal desire. We will examine this more behaviourist explanation later in the chapter.

It is possible that Freud's adult patients, who were mainly well-educated and middle class, were aware of his interest in certain topics. This may have affected their perspective, causing them to focus on childhood conflicts and sexuality during therapy, and to overlook other more important events.

The behaviourist approach

The behaviourist approach focuses on the idea that anxiety is a learned response. Individuals associate fear with a neutral stimulus through a process of **classical conditioning**. Alternatively, anxiety may develop because the response is reinforced (or rewarded) in some way. This is known as **operant conditioning**.

Study 2.3

AIM Watson and Rayner (1920) wanted to show how a phobia could be learned.

METHOD A nine-month-old baby, known as Albert, was tested for fear reaction to a number of stimuli, including a white rat, a rabbit, some cotton wool and a hammer hitting a steel bar just behind his head. Only the loud noise frightened him. Watson and Rayner then presented the rat to Albert and allowed him to stroke it. Whilst he was playing with the rat, Watson hit the hammer on the steel bar behind his head and frightened him.

RESULT After several pairings of the two stimuli, Albert developed a phobic response to the rat. He was fearful even when it was presented without the loud noise.

CONCLUSION Phobias are learned through a process of classical conditioning.

TWO PROCESS THEORY

Mowrer (1939) believed that there were two behavioural processes involved in anxiety disorders. First, the acquisition of fear is brought about by classical conditioning. Second, through a process of operant conditioning, the avoidance behaviour is maintained. By staying away from the feared object, anxiety levels drop. Avoidance behaviour is therefore positively reinforcing. For example, people with agoraphobia may have experienced a panic attack in a public place. They associate going out with a high level of anxiety and start to avoid it. This behaviour keeps their anxiety at an acceptable level and so avoidance is rewarding. By staying in, they reduce the likelihood of learning a new response and so the phobia continues. Anxiety levels are kept at manageable levels by the avoidance behaviour.

EVALUATIVE COMMENT

In Watson and Rayner's study the fear response was conditioned over several trials. In the real world, it is unlikely that two stimuli would be so systematically paired to produce the phobia.

Later attempts to replicate Watson and Rayner's experiment have not been successful. For example, Davison (1968) found that humans could not be classically conditioned to fear neutral stimuli, even when they were paired repeatedly with a painful electric shock.

Many phobic patients cannot remember unpleasant experiences with their feared stimulus. Conversely, many people have had unpleasant experiences and yet not developed a phobic response. For example, frightening events often happen in cars such as near misses, emergency stops or traffic accidents. However, cars are not a common object of specific phobias.

BEHAVIOURIST TREATMENTS

Behaviourist treatments are much less concerned about the underlying causes of the disorder than psychodynamic treatments, concentrating instead on helping the person learn new responses or behaviours to the things that make them anxious.

Study 2.4

AIM Jones (1924) wanted to show how a phobia could be successfully treated using behaviourist techniques.

METHOD He worked with Peter, a two-year-old boy who was frightened of a number of things, including rabbits. Jones put a rabbit in a cage in front of Peter while he was eating his lunch. Over 17 steps, the rabbit was brought closer to Peter, set free in the room and eventually sat on Peter's lunch tray.

RESULT Peter was no longer frightened of the rabbit.

CONCLUSION Classical conditioning can be successfully used to treat phobias.

The process used by Jones (1924) is known as **systematic desensitisation**. Behaviour therapists work with clients suffering from a variety of anxiety disorders to help them slowly and systematically overcome their anxiety. The first step is to teach the client relaxation techniques such as deep breathing. The therapist also educates the client about the body's stress response. For example, advising them that the human body works automatically to bring symptoms of anxiety under control. If the client experiences anxiety they should wait for a few minutes to allow it to subside.

The client then works with the therapist to draw up a **hierarchy** of anxiety-provoking events. This is a list of situations ranked from most difficult to cope with, down to least difficult. For example, a client with obsessive compulsive disorder who is fearful of contamination and washes compulsively might find gardening very stressful. Watching television might be the least stressful activity. The client is then asked to imagine being in these situations, starting with the least stressful. If they experience any anxiety during this process, they are asked to use their newly developed relaxation techniques or simply to wait for the feeling to disappear. The approach works through classical conditioning. The client is learning to associate a new response with a previously distressing stimulus. Eventually the client will be asked to experience the situations in real life. For the technique to be successful, the steps to recovery should be moderately challenging yet achievable.

REFLECTIVE Activity

Operant conditioning is also used in the treatment process. Imagine you are a psychologist working with a patient who has agoraphobia (a fear of open spaces). Draw up a treatment programme, lasting six weeks, to systematically desensitise your patient. Indicate where positive and negative reinforcement could be used.

EVALUATIVE COMMENT

Behaviour therapy can be very useful in treating anxiety but the client must be highly motivated to change and prepared to experience stressful situations. Many anxious people would find the regime too difficult to maintain.

The behaviourist approach doesn't look for underlying causes, and tends to focus on behaviour rather than thoughts and feelings. However, it has been successfully combined with cognitive approaches to create a new treatment method called cognitive behaviour therapy (CBT).

The cognitive approach

The cognitive theory of anxiety suggests that people become anxious because of their negative beliefs about themselves and the world. They have a tendency to perceive non-threatening situations as dangerous and anxiety provoking. Clark (in Hawton *et al.*, 1989) called this 'catastrophic misinterpretation'. For example, if you were talking with your friends and one of them yawned, you would probably conclude they'd had a late night. A person with an anxiety disorder is likely to interpret the same event very differently. For example, they might think 'I'm boring and everybody hates me.' They perceive an ordinary event as if it had terrible consequences. This creates or adds to any existing feelings of anxiety.

REFLECTIVE Activity

Think of some examples of catastrophic misinterpretations for the following anxiety disorders:

1. agoraphobia

2. social phobia

3. environmental phobia

4. situational phobia

5. OCD.

Beck *et al.* (1985) believed that anxious people often had negative thoughts about issues of acceptance, competence, responsibility, control and the physical symptoms of anxiety (see Figure 2.6).

Study 2.5

AIM Yun *et al.* (1997) wanted to investigate the role of cognitive processes in anxiety disorders. In particular, they wanted to find out how anxious patients interpreted the physical symptoms of anxiety.

METHOD They used questionnaires to measure and compare the interpretation of the physical symptoms of stress in three groups of participants. Group 1 consisted of participants suffering from anxiety disorders. Group 2 consisted of participants suffering from depression. Group 3 was a control group, with no psychological difficulties.

RESULT They found that those in the anxious group were more likely to interpret the physical symptoms of anxiety (such as an increased heart rate) as dangerous and life threatening than the other groups. Worries about the social consequences of the physical symptoms (such as embarrassment) were found in both the anxious and depressed groups.

CONCLUSION Negative thoughts about the physical symptoms of stress play an important role in the onset and maintenance of anxiety disorders. Both depressed and anxious participants have greater concerns about what others think about them than a control group.

Negative thoughts about:	Examples
acceptance (wanting others to accept you)	I must always please other people Everyone must like me
competence (being good at what you do)	If I make a mistake I am a total failure I have to be brilliant at everything I do
responsibility (looking after other people)	I take the blame for others' mistakes If people are unhappy it must be my fault
control (being in charge of your own life)	I'm the only one who can solve my problems No one else can help me
symptoms (heart racing, breathless etc.)	I am having a heart attack It's getting worse, I am dying

Figure 2.6: Typical cognitive distortions of patients with anxiety disorders

EVALUATIVE COMMENT

The cognitive approach concentrates on the negative thought processes that are evident in people with anxiety disorders However, it is not particularly interested in what causes someone to think in this way.

The approach also concentrates on the internal cognition of an individual, without taking into account any social or environmental factors. For example, King *et al.* (1999) found that people were less likely to suffer from post-traumatic stress disorder after a major trauma if they had a high level of social support available to them. Thought processes may be influenced by how much help is available to you.

COGNITIVE TREATMENTS

Cognitive therapy concentrates on the negative thought processes of an anxious individual and aims to directly challenge and change these catastrophic misrepresentations. First, the therapist will educate the client about the relationship between thought, feelings and behaviour. Beck *et al.* (1979) gave examples of how to achieve this. Clients are asked to imagine a person who heard a crash in another room, while alone in a house. The client is asked the following questions.

1. If the person thinks 'That must be a burglar' how would they feel and behave?

2. If the person thinks 'The window is open and the wind has blown something over' how would they feel and behave?

Clients should start to understand that negative thinking contributes to the anxiety disorder. If the client thinks in a positive way, they will feel and behave differently.

The client may also be taught a variety of distraction techniques to help them manage negative thoughts (Clark, in Hawton *et al.*, 1989). Some examples of these can be seen in Figure 2.7 on page 40. A series of questions (like the examples below) can also be used to help the client evaluate negative thoughts and replace them with more realistic ones.

1. What evidence do I have for this idea?

2. How would someone else think about the situation?

3. Are my judgements based on how I feel rather than what is happening?

4. What if it happens? So what?

Technique	Example
Focus on an object in the room	Describe it to yourself. How big is it? What colour is it? What is it made of? What is it for?
Sensory awareness	Focus on touch, sights, sounds, tastes and scent in your surroundings. What can you hear? Is it inside or outside the room?
Mental exercises	Counting back from 1000, thinking of animals beginning with each letter of the alphabet in turn
Pleasant memories or fantasies	Think of vivid, concrete memories of past success or enjoyment. Alternatively imagine what it would be like to win the lottery

Figure 2.7: Distraction techniques used in cognitive therapy with anxious patients

Towards the end of the therapy, the emphasis will move away from reducing the symptoms of anxiety, and towards maintaining the new ideas and thought processes. Clients may be asked to anticipate future setbacks and plan how they will overcome them.

EVALUATIVE COMMENT

Clark found that cognitive therapy was highly effective in the treatment of anxiety, particularly for patients prone to catastrophic misinterpretation of bodily symptoms such as increased heart rate. Many practitioners combine the cognitive and behavioural approaches to help the patient change both thoughts and behaviour.

However, as with any talking cure, the client must be quite articulate and be prepared to be challenged by the therapist. Clark (in Hawton *et al.*, 1989) acknowledges that it is sometimes difficult for anxious patients to identify their negative thoughts.

Effectiveness of treatments for anxiety

As we have seen, there are different explanations and treatments for anxiety disorders. The behaviourist approach has been successful in treating patients with anxiety. Salkovis and Kirk (in Hawton *et al.*, 1989) claim a 75 per cent improvement rate in the treatment of obsessive compulsive disorder by exposure techniques such as systematic desensitisation. However, treatment refusal and drop-out rates are also high (up to 50 per cent of those patients seeking help). This led Salkovis to recommend a combination of cognitive techniques with behavioural treatments. A collaborative relationship between the therapist and patient can be developed using a cognitive approach. This has been found to reduce treatment refusal.

Whilst drug treatments have been effective in reducing the symptoms of anxiety, Marks (1987) found a high incidence of troublesome side-effects. Also, when patients stop taking the medication, the symptoms may return. However, combining medication with behavioural techniques has been successful, because it helps the patient to feel more confident during exposure to anxiety-provoking situations.

Garfield (1980) reported that psychodynamic therapies are effective with well-educated, strongly motivated and confident people, suffering from light to moderate difficulties with anxiety. Researchers call this the YAVIS effect, since such people tend to be Young, Attractive, Verbal, Intelligent and Successful.

Some psychologists, such as Beitman *et al.* (1989), would argue that any effective therapy must be responsive to the individual client's needs. An experienced mental health care practitioner would tailor treatment methods to suit an individual patient. For example, a patient who had GAD might be offered a course of anxiolytic drugs and cognitive therapy.

2.4 Eating disorders

Preoccupation with body shape and weight is very common in many cultures. The desire to be slimmer has created a highly profitable diet industry in the western world, selling nutritional advice, exercise regimes and appetite-reducing drugs. Up to 90 per cent of women have been on a diet at some time in their lives (Ogden, 1992). The vast majority of dieters do not go on to develop the potentially dangerous relationship with food seen in eating disorders. However, it is perhaps not surprising that these disorders have primarily affected females.

Doctors' descriptions of patients with eating disorders were made as far back as the seventeenth century (Morton, 1694). However, these disorders did not appear in the *DSM* until 1980. A more recent edition made a distinction between anorexia nervosa and bulimia nervosa.

Symptoms and diagnosis of anorexia nervosa

Anorexia usually develops over a period of time, often (although not always) after dieting. The onset of symptoms can also follow a time of personal stress, such as being bullied at school (Stirling and Hellewell, 1999). The term anorexia nervosa means 'loss of appetite for nervous reasons'. However the term is misleading, as most sufferers do retain an appetite for food, which they rigorously attempt to control through starvation, over-exercising, vomiting and the excessive use of laxatives.

PHYSICAL SYMPTOMS

The physical symptoms of anorexia nervosa are:

- extreme weight loss in adults, failure to gain adequate weight in relation to growth in children and teenagers
- downy hair growth on the arms, back and face
- poor circulation and feeling cold
- dry, rough, discoloured skin
- low blood pressure
- disrupted menstrual cycles for females and, eventually, loss of fertility
- loss of bone mass and, eventually, osteoporosis (brittle bones).

PSYCHOLOGICAL SYMPTOMS

The psychological symptoms of anorexia nervosa include:

- Intense fear of gaining weight, even within the normal weight range. The sufferer can be constantly anxious about putting weight on. There is a tendency to assess self-worth almost exclusively in terms of weight and shape.
- Distorted perception of body shape and weight. Individuals overestimate their own body shape, believing they are bigger than they really are.
- Denial of the problem. Sufferers refuse to acknowledge that they are underweight or not eating.
- Changes in personality, and mood swings. Individuals may feel depressed or irritable and often concentration levels are affected. Progress at school or work can deteriorate.

BEHAVIOURAL SYMPTOMS

The behavioural symptoms of anorexia nervosa include:

- Rituals attached to eating such as cutting food into tiny pieces. Food causes high levels of anxiety in the anorexic. Rituals are undertaken in an attempt to control anxiety in a similar way to obsessive compulsive disorder.

- Restlessness and hyperactivity.

- Wearing baggy clothes to conceal weight loss.

- Vomiting, taking laxatives or exercising excessively.

DIAGNOSIS

The following four diagnostic criteria indicate anorexia nervosa.

1. Refusal to maintain normal body weight. Typically the person weighs less than 85 per cent of what is considered normal for their age and height.

2. Intense fear of gaining weight, which is not reduced by weight loss. Anorexics believe they can never be thin enough.

3. A distorted sense of their own body shape, believing certain parts of their body (usually stomach, bottom or thighs) are too fat.

4. For female patients, an absence of menstrual periods.

Davison and Neale (2001) state that anorexia nervosa usually begins in the early to late teens and is ten times more frequent in women than in men. In the UK the disorder affects up to 1 per cent of adolescent girls, more often occurring in the higher socioeconomic groups (Stirling and Hellewell, 1999). However, a review undertaken by the Eating Disorders Association (2000) identified that up to 10 per cent of people with eating disorders are now male. The incidence of anorexia in men appears to be growing.

Symptoms and diagnosis of bulimia nervosa

Bulimia nervosa involves rapid consumption of a large amount of food (a binge) followed by action to reduce the likelihood of weight gain, such as vomiting (a purge). Other non-purging behaviour can also be seen, such as over exercising or fasting.

PHYSICAL SYMPTOMS

The physical symptoms of bulimia nervosa are:

- frequent weight changes

- sore throat, gum disease and tooth decay caused by excessive vomiting

- swollen salivary glands

- poor skin condition

- irregular menstrual periods

- irregularities in heartbeat.

PSYCHOLOGICAL SYMPTOMS

The psychological symptoms of bulimia nervosa include:

• uncontrollable urges to eat vast amounts of food

• an obsession with food, which involves constant calorie checking

• distorted perception of body weight and shape

• mood swings

• anxiety and depression, low self-esteem and guilt.

BEHAVIOURAL SYMPTOMS

The behavioural symptoms of bulimia nervosa include:

• bingeing and vomiting

• excessive use of laxatives, diuretics or enemas

• excessive exercise

• secrecy and a reluctance to socialise

• shoplifting for food

• food disappearing unexpectedly.

DIAGNOSIS

Bulimia tends to develop later than anorexia, typically in young adulthood. A substantial minority of sufferers will also abuse drugs and alcohol (Stirling and Hellewell, 1999). Again, bulimia affects mainly women, with men representing only 5 per cent of reported cases. It tends to affect people in the higher socioeconomic groups. Bulimia is more common than anorexia, affecting about 3 per cent of the population. For a diagnosis to be made, episodes of bingeing and purging should occur twice a week for three months.

Societal explanations for eating disorders

This approach looks to cultural pressures as an explanation for eating disorders. Over the past 50 years the 'ideal' body shape for women has changed in western society, with a steady progression towards increasing thinness. The societal explanation acknowledges the importance of social influences on an individual's psychology. Social learning theory (see Chapter 4 in *Introducing Psychology*) states that people learn through observation and imitation of role models. In addition, **positive reinforcement** increases the likelihood of imitation. Many young women look to the media for information about what is desirable. If thinness appears to be highly valued then the media is positively reinforcing a particular body size and shape.

Study 2.6

AIM Ogden (1992) looked for evidence that the ideal shape for women has become slimmer.

METHOD The physical features of female fashion models recruited by an agency in London from 1967–1987 were analysed. The researchers examined the models' height, bust, waist and hip measurements.

RESULT Over the 20-year period, models became taller, with a decrease in hip and bust measurements relative to waist size.

CONCLUSION Ogden concluded that the ideal female shape had become more **androgynous** (could be either male or female) and that this has an effect on how women perceive their own body shape.

Bemis (1978) suggests that eating disorders arise from attempts by young women to conform to a stereotyped and unrealistic body shape shown in magazines, television, films and adverts. Anorexia and bulimia are much more common in western societies where thinness is regarded as desirable.

Western society's attitude towards fatness has also grown increasingly negative. De Jong and Kleck (1986) found that obese people are seen as less smart, more lonely, and greedy for the affection of others.

Study 2.7

AIM Furnham and Baguma (1994) investigated cross-cultural differences in ideal body shape.

METHOD Ugandan and British college students were asked to rate the attractiveness of drawings of nudes ranging from very thin to very obese.

RESULT Ugandan students rated the obese females as more attractive than the British students did.

CONCLUSION British attitudes to obesity are more negative. This may contribute to the higher incidence of eating disorders in the United Kingdom.

Some professions have a higher incidence of eating disorders than others

REFLECTIVE Activity

Look through some recent copies of magazines aimed at young people. What kinds of images are shown? Is there any difference in the types of article aimed at young men compared to young women? Can you explain why there is now a slow but steady increase in the number of men being diagnosed with eating disorders?

EVALUATIVE COMMENT

Social pressures appear to contribute to the onset of eating disorders. They are certainly more common amongst people who might be expected to be concerned about their appearance, such as dancers or models (Garner et al., 1980)

As we are all subject to the same cultural pressures, eating disorders such as anorexia and bulimia should be more widespread. Instead, there is an increase in the number of overweight people, with 16 per cent of women categorised as obese (Ogden, 1992). There must be other contributory factors, such as family background or biology.

Family pressures

Minuchin et al. (1975) proposed that the family had an important role in the development of eating disorders. He used the term **enmeshed family** to describe the way family members relate to each other. Parents in these kinds of families tend to speak for the child, believing that they know exactly how the child feels. Minuchin thought this over-involvement and protectiveness promoted the development of eating disorders. During adolescence, when a young person is striving for **autonomy**, the parents tend not to acknowledge or encourage increased independence. As a consequence, the child tries to gain some sense of control by refusing to eat, or bingeing and purging.

Minuchin gathered evidence for his theory by working with patients with eating disorders and their families. He developed a treatment method known as family therapy, claiming that recovery could only occur if the whole family was helped to communicate more effectively.

Research has focused on the relationship dynamics within the family.

Study 2.8

AIM Humphrey (1989) investigated the way families with an anorexic daughter communicated.

METHOD He used the structural analysis of social behaviour (SASB), which is a method used to analyse the interactions of families.

RESULT Parents' communication with anorexic daughters consisted of double messages. For example, they might offer verbal affection but at the same time dismiss the daughter's thoughts and feelings. The daughter would therefore be confused and swing between expressing herself and submitting to the parents' wishes.

CONCLUSION Interaction is unusual in families with anorexic children. Mixed messages caused confusion in the children, which may be why anorexia develops.

EVALUATIVE COMMENT

One problem with research into family dynamics is that it happens after diagnosis of the eating disorder. The communication within the family may have changed because one member has become ill. It is therefore not possible to state causality. Woodside *et al.* (1995) found that family functioning improved after treatment of the patient. His study supports the idea that eating disorders cause family problems, rather than the other way round.

Alternatively, van den Broucke *et al.* (1995) found that parents of children with eating disorders did not appear to be very different from a control group. In their observational study, both groups gave similar amounts of positive and negative messages to their children.

Biological explanations

Both anorexia and bulimia run in families. Strober *et al.* (1990) found that first-degree relatives (parents) of anorexic daughters were four times more likely than average to have the disorder themselves. Researchers have again turned to twin studies to find evidence of a genetic link. For example, Holland (1984) found a higher concordance rate for eating disorders in identical twins (55 per cent) than non-identical twins. This indicates that genetics are implicated in anorexia. However, the concordance rate is not 100 per cent and therefore other factors must also be involved.

REFLECTIVE Activity

You should be able to evaluate twin studies research. Look back at Study 2.1 in this chapter to help you.

A second possible biological explanation has centred on the role of endogenous opiods. These are substances made by the body to suppress appetite, reduce pain and enhance mood. During starvation, endogenous opiods are produced, which can result in feelings of euphoria. A person with anorexia will have high levels of these substances. This might explain why they are motivated to continue abstaining from food. Marrazi *et al.* (1986) found that endogenous opiods are also released during excessive exercise, which many anorexics use to control weight gain. Brewerton *et al.* (1992) found low levels of endogenous opiods in patients with bulimia. This might explain why they experience extreme craving for food, resulting in binge eating.

A third biological explanation has concentrated on the role of neurotransmitters (see page 32). Several studies have indicated low levels of **serotonin** in the brains of patients with eating disorders (see Chapter 3). This substance is also involved in the regulation of appetite, and research has shown a connection between low serotonin levels in the brain and the incidence of bulimia.

Study 2.9

AIM Smith *et al.* (1999) wanted to investigate the role of serotonin in bulimia nervosa.

METHOD Patients who had recovered from bulimia nervosa had their serotonin levels reduced using a drug treatment. The researchers closely monitored any changes in mood and behaviour.

RESULT Patients reported an increase in negative thoughts about their body as serotonin levels dropped. For example, they began to worry about feeling fat.

CONCLUSION Low levels of the neurotransmitter may be implicated in the onset of bulimia nervosa.

Support for this theory also comes from an effective treatment for bulimia. Antidepressant drugs that increase serotonin can lead to dramatic reductions in the frequency of binge eating (Stirling and Hellewell, 1999).

EVALUATIVE COMMENT

Research will continue into the role of biochemistry in eating disorders. However, the focus on hunger, eating and appetite fails to acknowledge other more psychological symptoms in eating disorders, such as intense fear of being fat, or behavioural symptoms such as ritualistic eating patterns.

Disturbances in neurotransmitter function have also been found in mood disorders (see Chapter 3). Research is as yet unable to explain why low serotonin levels in the brain lead to bulimia in some people and unipolar depression in others. It is likely that cultural influences may have an impact.

Cognitive explanations

Cognitive theories emphasise the thought processes of a person with an eating disorder – in particular, over-concern with the importance of body weight and shape. Beck *et al.* (1979) found that people who were having psychological difficulties in life often had unrealistic expectations about themselves (see Chapter 3). Garner and Bemis (1982) have applied some of Beck's theory to eating disorders. Figure 2.9 shows some typical cognitive distortions of patients with anorexia or bulimia nervosa.

Fairburn (in Hawton *et al.*, 1989) found that most patients with eating disorders admit they are unlikely ever to be completely satisfied with their shape and weight. If these patients continue to determine their self-worth through body shape, they are likely to continually suffer from eating disorders and remain unhappy.

These distorted thought processes lead the patient to adopt strict, inflexible dietary rules. If the rules are broken – for example, by eating the wrong type of food – the sufferer will experience a sense of failure and a decrease in self-esteem. In an attempt to feel better, the patient embarks on an even more rigorous diet. Losing weight provides the patient with an objective measure of success.

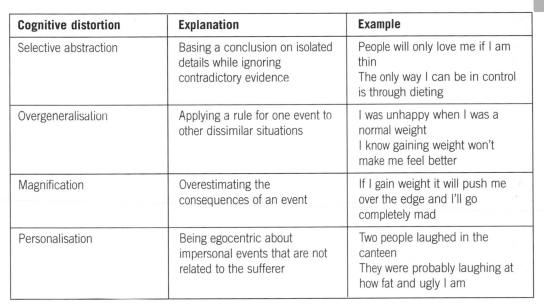

Cognitive distortion	Explanation	Example
Selective abstraction	Basing a conclusion on isolated details while ignoring contradictory evidence	People will only love me if I am thin The only way I can be in control is through dieting
Overgeneralisation	Applying a rule for one event to other dissimilar situations	I was unhappy when I was a normal weight I know gaining weight won't make me feel better
Magnification	Overestimating the consequences of an event	If I gain weight it will push me over the edge and I'll go completely mad
Personalisation	Being egocentric about impersonal events that are not related to the sufferer	Two people laughed in the canteen They were probably laughing at how fat and ugly I am

Figure 2.9: Typical cognitive distortions of patients with anorexia and bulimia nervosa

REFLECTIVE Activity

Cognitive theorists often combine the approach with behavioural explanations. Look back at the last paragraph and identify how a patient's behaviour can be explained by using the terms 'negative' and 'positive' reinforcement.

People with anorexia and bulimia not only have distorted attitudes about the importance of body shape, they are also more likely to overestimate their own shape and size.

Study 2.10

AIM Zellner *et al.* (1989) investigated women's assessments of their own body size.

METHOD Female participants were given a questionnaire to assess whether they had a distorted attitude towards eating. Women with high scores or low scores were then assessed on their own body size, using line drawings of women with varying body weights. Participants were asked to pick the one closest to their own body shape and choose an ideal figure.

RESULT High scorers overestimated their own body size and chose a very thin figure as their ideal when compared with low scorers.

CONCLUSION Cognitive distortion in women with eating disorders includes an over-assessment of their own size, as well as over-concern with body weight. Even when anorexics are reduced to skin and bones they still claim to be 'too fat'.

EVALUATIVE COMMENT

While there is plenty of evidence to demonstrate cognitive distortion in those diagnosed with an eating disorder, the approach does not explain where these thoughts originated. Thompson *et al.* (1995) found that criticism from peers and parents, about being overweight was positively correlated with disturbed body image. Some studies have indicated that reports of childhood physical or sexual abuse are higher than normal among patients with eating disorders (Deep *et al.*, 1999). Other research has highlighted the role of stress such as exam pressure or relationship problems. The cognitive approach ignores these external, environmental causes.

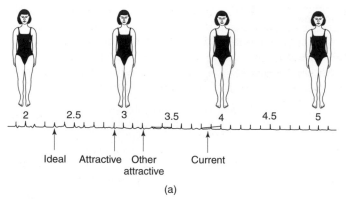

Figure 2.10:
High scorers
overestimated their
own size and would
ideally be very thin

(a)

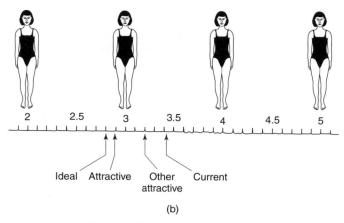

(b)

However, the cognitive explanation does provide a means of treating anorexia and bulimia, which is currently in use, with some success (see below).

2.5 Treatments for eating disorders

There are currently several treatment methods available to help individuals with eating disorders, including weight restoration, behaviour therapy and cognitive treatments. Research into which is the most effective treatment is ongoing.

Weight restoration

For some patients with anorexia, weight loss is so severe that they have to be admitted to hospital for treatment. If patients are underweight by 60 per cent for their age, sex and height, and are refusing treatment, they can be admitted to hospital without their consent under the Mental Health Act (see Chapter 4).

While under supervision on the ward, patients are slowly introduced to eating regular meals and snacks (Fairburn, in Hawton *et al.*, 1989). It usually takes about two weeks for patients to be able to physically cope with a normal quantity of food. A weekly weight gain target is set of around 1.5 kilograms. To achieve this weight gain, the patient must eat between 3000 and 5000 calories a day. This would require abnormally large or frequent meals, so high-calorie drinks and snacks are often given in addition to normal meals. Patients are usually weighed each day and monitored closely to ensure that food is not being hidden away or vomited. Patients are encouraged to talk to nursing staff throughout the treatment, about their distress and resistance to weight gain.

The doctors and nursing staff will negotiate with the patient to agree on a satisfactory target weight. Sometimes, this might be the weight they were before they became ill. However, for patients who have been ill for many years, it is often difficult to identify a 'natural' weight. Generally, the target weight will be at least 90 per cent of the average for the height, sex and age of the patient. This should allow normal hormonal functioning to return and also represent a body size at which eating without dieting is possible. Once patients enter the target weight range, the high-calorie supplements are phased out.

This type of in-patient weight restoration takes between two and three months to complete. Sometimes, the treatment will include a programme of behaviour therapy (see page 50).

The patient usually remains on the ward for between two and four weeks after reaching their target weight. The transition from in-patient to out-patient care must be very carefully managed to avoid relapse, and may involve some form of ongoing psychotherapy (see page 51).

Patients who are less dangerously underweight can take part in weight restoration programmes as out-patients. Initial appointments at the hospital will be very frequent to get the

---

The purpose of monitoring is to provide a detailed picture of your eating habits. It is central to treatment. At first, writing down everything you eat may seem inconvenient and irritating, but soon it becomes second nature and of obvious value.

Here is a sample monitoring sheet of a patient with bulimia.

Time	Food and liquid consumed	Place	Bulimic episode (B)	Vomiting or laxative use (V or L)	Circumstances
7.45	1 apple 1 grapefruit 1 black coffee	Kitchen			Feel hungry and a bit depressed
9.00	3 egg sandwiches 2 doughnuts 3 bars of chocolate	Work	B		Bought more food from the canteen, feel terrible, bound to be a bad day
9.30	1 doughnut 1 cup tea 4 bags of crisps	Work	B	V	I have put on weight, started to cry, must do something
9.50	1 diet coke	Work			Must not eat again today
1.00	2 glasses of water			L	Weighed myself I have put on weight, I wish I was dead

A separate sheet (or sheets) should be used for each day with the date and day of the week noted at the top. Every treatment interview will include a careful review of your monitoring sheets. You must therefore remember to bring them with you.

Figure 2.11: Instructions for monitoring food intake

weight gain started (for example, three times a week). Patients monitor their own food intake (see Figure 2.11) but weight gain is monitored by hospital staff. The expected weight gain for out-patients is lower than for in-patients, at about 0.5 kg per week. During their appointments, patients are given help and advice about their diet. They are encouraged to eat regular meals and in the initial stages they may need energy-rich supplements. Out-patient care may also involve some form of psychotherapy, usually cognitive (see page 51).

EVALUATIVE COMMENT

Weight restoration within hospital settings can be life-saving for dangerously underweight anorexics. Most of the physical complications of anorexia nervosa can be reversed if weight is restored. Unfortunately, keeping the weight on after the patient is discharged is more problematic. Despite out-patient care, many patients relapse and require further hospital treatment. This may be because the treatment focuses mainly on the physical symptoms rather than the psychological causes of the disorder.

Weight restoration concentrates solely on the individual patient and the problem is defined within the sufferer. Therapists such as Minuchin et al. (1975) argue that eating disorders are an interpersonal problem – they occur as a result of communication difficulties between family members. Treatment should therefore include the whole family rather than just the anorexic individual.

Behavioural therapy

This type of treatment is often used within weight restoration programmes. The belief is that patients can learn new and more adaptive ways of responding to food.

Study 2.11

AIM Hsu (1990) reported on the use of a strict operant conditioning technique to treat patients with anorexia.

METHOD Patients were isolated as much as possible. Social contact was given when the patient ate a meal. Rewards, such as access to television, having visitors or going outside for a walk, were given when the patient gained weight.

RESULT The programme was successful. Patients ate more regularly and gained weight.

CONCLUSION Operant conditioning treatments, using positive reinforcement for appropriate behaviour, can help the weight restoration process.

More lenient approaches have used **negative reinforcement**. Touyz et al. (1984) recommended that staff and patients negotiate a weekly weight gain. Patients should be given full access to social contact and advised that if their weight doesn't increase after four days, they will be required to take 'bed rest' for three days. During this time they will be more closely monitored and not allowed to exercise. Touyz argued that this approach helped the patient to develop a sense of control over their own treatment and was as effective as stricter programmes. Behaviour therapy is also used outside the hospital setting, in individual therapy sessions.

EVALUATIVE COMMENT

Behaviour therapy regimes have advantages. They are easily understood by staff, family and patients, and are straightforward to carry out. However, critics of strict operant conditioning argue that it is degrading for patients to have their privileges taken away and difficult to maintain outside the hospital ward.

Today, most therapists accept that as well as changing behaviour, clients must also be helped to change the way they think. Cognitive behavioural therapy has proved effective, particularly for treating patients with bulimia nervosa.

REFLECTIVE Activity

Can you identify the cognitive processes involved in bulimia? What types of negative thoughts might lead to bingeing? What types of negative thoughts might lead to purging? How could a therapist help to change these negative thoughts?

Cognitive treatments

Patients with either anorexia or bulimia nervosa have extreme concerns about shape and weight. Fairburn and Cooper (in Hawton *et al.*, 1989) highlight how these concerns mean patients begin to judge their self-worth almost exclusively in terms of their ability to control their food intake and weight. These over-valued ideas about thinness must be challenged if the patient is to make a full and lasting recovery. Thought modification is one of the major goals of cognitive treatments for eating disorders. Beck *et al.* (1979) called this process **cognitive restructuring** (see Chapter 4).

Study 2.12

AIM Fairburn (1985) applied cognitive restructuring techniques to the treatment of bulimia nervosa.

METHOD Patients were given individual cognitive treatments for about five months. There were three stages to the therapy.

In Stage 1 the cognitive explanation for bulimia was given to the patient. They were asked to fill in a food diary (see Figure 2.11). This helped the therapist to see some of the patient's negative thoughts about themselves.

The emphasis of Stage 2 was on examining and replacing the problematic thoughts and attitudes revealed by the food diary. It involved providing factual information on topics such as the physical consequences of bulimia, the ineffectiveness of vomiting and using laxatives to control weight, and the adverse effects of dieting. The main point stressed by the therapist was that dieting encouraged over-eating. For example, bulimic patients often embark on strict and rigid diets that are impossible to maintain. As a result, at some stage they break their diet. This increases negative thoughts about their poor self-control. The aim of this stage is for the patient to reach their own conclusion that dieting does not work.

In Stage 3 the focus was on maintaining the new thought processes. For example, the patient would be asked to prepare a written plan, for dealing with future times when they sense that eating is becoming a problem.

RESULT The findings indicated that patients benefited from this type of treatment in the short term, although long-term follow up has not been undertaken.

CONCLUSION Cognitive restructuring techniques can be used successfully to treat patients with bulimia nervosa.

EVALUATIVE COMMENT

Cognitive treatments for bulimia have been successful in the short term. When combined with behavioural techniques, Whittal *et al.* (1999) found that patients fared better with cognitive behavioural therapy than any drug treatments available. However, more long-term research is

needed to see if the improvements are permanent. In anorexia, the approach has yet to be significantly evaluated.

One difficulty with the cognitive approach is that the individual may be using the eating disorder to experience some sense of control. Minuchin *et al.* (1975) believed that enmeshed families, who were very controlling, contributed to the onset of the disorder. The cognitive approach involves a direct challenge of the patient's thought processes, which may be interpreted by the patient as further interference and control. Additionally, the cognitive approach focuses on the individual sufferer and ignores their social environment.

2.6 Effectiveness of treatments

Around 70 per cent of people with eating disorders eventually get better (Davison and Neale, 2001). However, recovery may take between six and seven years, with frequent relapses. For anorexics, failure to maintain a healthy body weight can have a serious impact on the sufferer's physical health. Where menstrual abnormalities are present over a period of time, there may be permanent infertility. Anorexia can be a life-threatening illness and death rates are twice as high for anorexia as for any other psychological disorder. Weight restoration can therefore be seen as a highly effective treatment for anorexia because it halts the physical consequences of acute starvation. However, other more psychological treatments such as cognitive behavioural therapy may be needed to ensure that the weight gain is maintained.

Researchers like Minuchin *et al.* (1975), as we have seen, argue that anorexia is not an individual problem but the result of interpersonal problems within a family. He recommended that treatment included the whole family and not just the anorexic. Fairburn and Cooper (in Hawton *et al.*, 1989) outline an effective cognitive behavioural treatment but also stress the importance of family involvement. In particular, family members must be advised of the patient's goals, and be included in strategies to strengthen the patient's motivation.

Bulimia is often more difficult to detect than anorexia because the sufferer usually maintains a near normal body weight. Bingeing and purging tend to occur in secret. Treatment for bulimia may therefore be delayed, causing the symptoms to get worse over a long period of time. Rowan (2002) found that a common time for bulimic women to seek help is when they are planning to start a family and are concerned about the possible effects on having a baby.

Whilst there has been some success with antidepressants as a treatment for bulimia, few patients make a complete recovery, and disturbed attitudes to shape and weight tend to persist. A combination of cognitive and behavioural therapy has been effective in challenging these faulty perceptions. However, further research is needed to establish if the improvement is maintained over time.

Answers to the phobias quiz
1(c) 2(b) 3(c) 4(b) 5(c) 6(d) 7(a) 8(d) 9(c) 10(b)

2.7 Sample questions

SAMPLE QUESTION

(a) Identify three symptoms associated with post-traumatic stress disorder.

(AO1 = 3)   *(3 marks)*

(b) Outline and discuss one type of treatment for post-traumatic stress disorder.

(AO1 = 2, AO2 = 3)   *(5 marks)*

(c) Alex was at university and feeling quite unwell. One morning he went to the doctor to explain how he felt:

'I've always been very anxious and tense but lately I've become much worse and I feel angry all the time. I worry constantly that things might happen, such as having an incurable disease. I can't sleep and I often feel dizzy and feel breathless. I'm afraid I can no longer cope.'

Alex was subsequently diagnosed as suffering from generalised anxiety disorder.

Identify and discuss two explanations that might account for generalised anxiety disorder such as that suffered by Alex. Refer to empirical evidence in your answer.

(AO1 = 5, AO2 = 7)   *(12 marks)*

Total AO1 marks = 10 Total AO2 marks = 10 Total = 20 marks

QUESTIONS, ANSWERS AND COMMENTS

(a) Give one atypical behaviour associated with each of the following types of phobia: (i) agoraphobia, (ii) social phobia, (iii) specific phobia.

(AO1 = 3)   *(3 marks)*

(b) Compare and contrast the symptoms of anorexia nervosa and bulimia nervosa.

(AO1 = 2, AO2 = 3)   *(5 marks)*

(c)   Jenny was 16 years old and had just started her AS-level course when her parents noticed a change in her. She had always been sensitive but was now very moody and easily offended. She became very conscious of her weight and began skipping meals.

Her parents tried to persuade her she was not overweight but she became very socially withdrawn and would not eat in front of them. Her mother found food wrapped up and thrown in the bin, and insisted on taking Jenny to the doctor. She was diagnosed as suffering from anorexia nervosa.

Discuss two explanations of Jenny's anorexia nervosa. Refer to theory and evidence in your answer.

(AO1 = 5, AO2 = 7)   *(12 marks)*

Total AO1 marks = 10 Total AO2 marks = 10 Total = 20 marks

Answer to (a)

(i) Agoraphobia is a fear of the market-place so the person will not go out.

(ii) A person with social phobia will avoid social situations in case they do something embarrassing.

(iii) This is a fear of a specific object or thing – for example, a fear of snakes.

Comment: 2 marks awarded for this answer. No mark given for (iii) as the answer provides a definition and not a type of behaviour.

Answer to (b)

Anorexia nervosa is characterised by a severe weight loss and fear of weight gain. The patient will also stop having periods, and may often feel cold. The patient controls weight gain by eating very little, exercising and vomiting. A bulimia sufferer will also have a fear of weight gain but they do not starve themselves. They have bouts of over-eating known as binges, followed by action to reduce the likelihood of weight gain such as vomiting. This is known as purging. Both eating disorders may involve being sick but an anorexic would not binge. A bulimic would not necessarily be underweight whereas an anorexic would.

Comment: 2 marks (AO1) awarded for accurate description of the symptoms, and 3 marks (AO2) for clearly comparing and differentiating between the disorders.

Answer to (c)

Jenny may have developed anorexia nervosa as a result of poor communication within her family. Minuchin *et al.* (1975) argued that family pressures caused anorexia. He used the term enmeshed family to describe the way a family might interact. Parents in these families speak for the child and take control over it. During adolescence a teenager will try to be independent but the enmeshed family will try to retain control. This might cause the child to develop an eating disorder. Humphrey (1989) investigated the way families interact and found that parents of anorexic daughters did give out confusing messages. The child was confused about how to respond. Humphrey's study shows that family interaction is unusual. A problem with this study is that it took place after diagnosis, so the strange communication could have been the result of anorexia occurring rather than the cause of it.

Another explanation for anorexia is social pressures. In western society fatness is seen to be negative and undesirable. Research compared British and Ugandan college students' attitudes to body shape. They were asked to rate the attractiveness of drawings of nudes ranging from thin to very fat. Ugandans preferred the fuller figures and found them more attractive than British students did. This shows that in Britain we have negative attitudes to a larger body shape. This is why people become anorexic. Also lots of role models in the media are very thin. Young women are likely to imitate these role models according to social learning theory. A difficulty with this idea is that more people are overweight in Britain than anorexic so it's obviously not affecting us all. There must be other reasons such as biology or cognitive processes.

There is no one answer to what causes anorexia. It must be a combination of family and social pressures.

Comment: The answer makes a good attempt at describing two explanations and provides evidence to support them (5 marks awarded for AO1). There has been an attempt at analysis and evaluation although this is limited to two ideas. Although other explanations are briefly mentioned (biology and cognition) these should be explained more fully to achieve a higher mark (4 marks awarded for AO2). Overall, 9 marks awarded, which denotes a good to average answer.

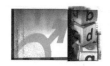

2.8 FURTHER READING

Introductory texts

Davison, G.C. & Neale, J.M. 2001: **Abnormal Psychology**. 8th Ed. Wiley, New York

Gross, R. & McIlveen, R. 2000: **Psychopathology**. Hodder & Stoughton, London

Stirling, J.D. & Hellewell, S.E. 1999: **Psychopathology, Atypical Development and Abnormal Behaviour**. Routledge, London and New York

Specialist sources

Chisholm, K. 2002: **Hungry Hell: What it's Really Like to be Anorexic**. Short Books, London

Hawton, K., Salkovis, P.M., Kirk, J. & Clark, D.M. 1989: **Cognitive Behaviour Therapy for Psychiatric Problems**. Oxford Medical Publications, Oxford

Ogden, J. 1992: **Fat Chance: The Myth of Dieting Explained**. Routledge, London

Useful websites

www.edauk.com The eating disorders association

www.news.bbc.co.uk Go to health/medical notes for up-to-date articles on all aspects of mental health

www.sane.org.uk Useful information on anxiety disorders

3
Mood disorders and schizophrenia

3.1 Introduction

Most people will experience mood changes from time to time. Temporary changes in emotion, thoughts and behaviour are normal. For example, you may feel low and stressed during revision but become elated when your results are announced. You go out to celebrate, spend too much money, act impulsively and regret your behaviour the following day!

Less frequently, people experience severe, sometimes long-term, mood and behaviour changes, requiring the help of a mental health professional. Doctors and psychiatrists use a manual, listing symptoms, to make a diagnosis. The *International Classification of Disease, Injuries and Causes of Death (ICD)*, used in Europe and the UK, covers both physical and mental disorders. The *Diagnostic and Statistical Manual (DSM)*, used extensively in the USA, covers only mental disorders. Information about mental health problems is very similar in each of the two publications (see Chapter 1).

3.2 Unipolar and bipolar depression

One mood disorder listed in both the *DSM* and the *ICD* is unipolar depression. This is the term used when a person's mood changes from normal to depressed. It can range from mild to severe, and is categorised as a neurosis. People suffering from unipolar depression are usually aware of their mood change and will either spontaneously recover or voluntarily seek help.

A second type of depressive illness is bipolar disorder. Bipolar disorder is characterised by a mood swing from a very low, depressed state to a mania. About one in ten people diagnosed with clinical depression find that when the depression lifts, they enter a period of extreme elation known as mania. Bipolar disorder is therefore characterised by mood swings. During the manic phase the person may lose touch with reality and the illness is therefore categorised as a psychosis.

Symptoms of unipolar depression

Depression can affect the thoughts (cognition), feelings (emotion), behaviour and physical well-being of an individual.

COGNITIVE SYMPTOMS

The thought processes of a depressed person are often impaired. Memory and concentration can be affected. They can find it difficult to think in a positive way about themselves or their future. Sometimes, the person will experience persistent worrying without any obvious cause. They may think about committing suicide.

EMOTIONAL SYMPTOMS

A depressed person often has feelings of sadness and despair. Some people might experience an absence of feelings and describe themselves as 'empty'. They may have no interest or pleasure in everyday activities, as if they 'can't be bothered'. Feelings of excessive guilt, about real or imagined events, can also occur.

BEHAVIOURAL SYMPTOMS

A severely depressed person can stop socialising, lose interest in sex and stop taking care of themself. Everyday activities may take much longer to complete. They may attempt suicide.

PHYSICAL SYMPTOMS

Doctors believe that around 40 per cent of people suffering with depression visit their surgery for the first time because of physical symptoms. These include aches and pains, a lack of energy, palpitations, headaches and stomach upsets. Sleep disturbance is another possible symptom. There can be a loss of appetite and weight.

Diagnosis of unipolar depression

Unipolar depression may appear gradually or suddenly. It occurs in all social classes and at all ages, from childhood to old age. The severe forms are more common in middle and old age although there has been a steady increase in depressive illnesses amongst people in their twenties and thirties. Before a diagnosis of depression can be made, the symptoms (which might be a combination of those listed) should have lasted for at least two weeks.

EVALUATIVE COMMENT

While the *DSM* and *ICD* enable practitioners to diagnose a mood disorder on the basis of symptoms experienced, there are no physical tests to establish signs of disease or illness. For example, a broken bone can be confirmed by using an x-ray. Mental health problems are more difficult to diagnose because they are based on self-report from the patient (see Chapter 1).

Another important difference between diagnosing physical illness and mental disorder is the aetiology (cause of the disease). Physical illnesses, like an outbreak of Legionnaire's disease, can be traced to the cause – most recently in the UK, a faulty air-conditioning system. As you will see throughout this chapter it is much more problematic for mental health practitioners to establish (or agree on) the causes of the disorder.

REFLECTIVE Activity

There are gender differences in the incidence of unipolar depression. In Britain 3–4 per cent of men, compared to 7–8 per cent of women, suffer from moderate to severe depression at any one time. However, the male suicide rate is almost three times as high as the female rate.

Why do you think this is? (Remembering some of the theories from Explaining Gender at AS level may help you.)

1 in 4 people will experience mental distress at some point in their life

www.mind.org.uk

Mind: Making a Difference

"Having a mental health problem is worse than having a criminal record. I found I couldn't concentrate, was getting more tired and I started sleeping through my spare time. It got to the point where I was called into the Chairman's office and told they couldn't go on with the situation anymore and asked me to leave there and then. Shortly after that my partner of two years left me.

I've travelled a journey and the message is that people do get better, there is hope and you can live a meaningful life."

Martin, who received help and support from Mind

Mind
The Mental Health Charity
Registered Charity No. 219830

Recent mental health campaigns have tried to reach young people (MIND, 2003)

Symptoms of bipolar disorder

When depressed, the sufferer experiences similar symptoms to those present in unipolar disorder. The symptoms described below appear when the person enters the manic phase.

COGNITIVE

The thought processes of a person in a manic state can be quite severely disrupted. They can have delusional ideas, believing, for example, they are a famous person. This is known as a grandiose delusion. They may think that other people are trying to harm or kill them. This is known as a persecutory delusion. Sometimes the person may hear voices inside their head or have visual hallucinations. They may also make reckless and irrational decisions, showing little regard for the effect of these on others.

EMOTIONAL

A person in the manic state will feel marvellous! They will therefore strongly deny that there is anything wrong with them, because they feel so good. They may become irritable with those around them who attempt to intervene. There can be a loss of social inhibitions and a lack of guilt.

BEHAVIOURAL

There is often a marked increase in work, sexual and social activity. The person may become more talkative and speak faster. They may become reckless, with negative consequences.

PHYSICAL

During this phase the person will tend to sleep very little and have an increase in energy levels.

DIAGNOSIS OF BIPOLAR DEPRESSION

This disorder, which is sometimes called manic depression, affects about five people in a thousand, with equal numbers of men and women. Symptoms of both depression and mania must have been experienced for a diagnosis to be made. Patients may be unaware that there is anything wrong during the manic phase. In serious cases they may be admitted to a psychiatric unit for treatment without their consent, under an Assessment Order of Section 2 of the Mental Health Act 1983 (see Chapter 4).

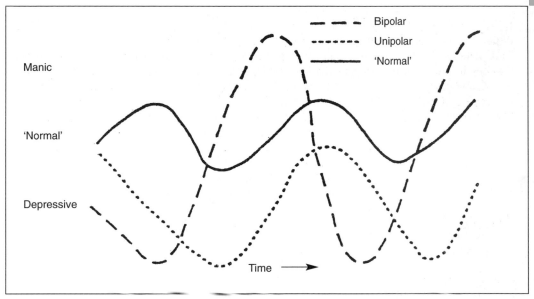

Figure 3.3: Line graph to show mood changes in normal functioning, unipolar and bipolar depression

REFLECTIVE Activity

Mental health is the only area of medicine able to legally treat adult patients without their consent. What effect do you think this might have on the thoughts (cognition), feelings (emotion) and behaviour of a patient? Look back at some of the symptoms of unipolar disorder to help you.

3.3 Seasonally affective disorder

Seasonally affective disorder (SAD) is a type of depression occurring in the winter months. For some people the illness is very severe, preventing them from functioning normally. SAD can begin at any age, but the main age of onset is between 18 to 30 years. It can be either unipolar or bipolar. Unipolar SAD will end in spring with a return to normal functioning. With bipolar SAD, the sufferer enters a manic phase when winter ends. The condition is usually diagnosed when the person has had three or more consecutive winters of symptoms.

The pineal gland in the brain secretes a hormone called melatonin when it begins to get dark outside. The hormone acts to make us feel drowsy and ready for sleep. This biological influence may explain why SAD occurs. People who are sensitive to seasonal changes in the intensity and duration of daylight may be more prone to SAD.

Study 3.1

AIM Terman (1988) tried to find evidence that a reduction in daylight hours contributed to SAD.

METHOD He compared the incidence of depression in two parts of America where daylight hours were different.

RESULT He found 10 per cent of people living in New Hampshire, where the winter days are very short, suffered from SAD. In Florida, which has more daylight during winter, the incidence dropped to 2 per cent.

CONCLUSION The difference in daylight hours was a contributory factor in the onset of seasonally affective disorder.

EVALUATIVE COMMENT

Other studies have highlighted the impact of changes in geomagnetism as an explanation for SAD. Whittel (1995) noted that suicide rates for young people in Alaska are six times higher than the US average. He suggests that the *aurora borealis* (Northern Lights) over Alaska, which causes changes in direction of the magnetic field, may be a contributory factor.

Support for the importance of daylight is evidenced in the success of a treatment method known as *phototherapy*. Barlow and Durand (1995) found the condition can be eased by exposure to very bright light, at least ten times the intensity of the domestic light bulb, for up to two hours a day. Light boxes have been developed for this purpose, but are not yet available on the NHS. They cost about £100. However, phototherapy is a time-consuming and often inconvenient treatment method. It can cause headaches and eye strain in some people (Syal, 1997). Another, even more expensive, alternative is to head for sunnier climes during winter!

REFLECTIVE Activity

While biological processes may be involved in the onset of SAD, other factors may also be involved. For example, students (and teachers) have a long holiday during the summer, which might contribute to their well-being. List ten other reasons why people tend to feel happier in summer.

Wearing fewer clothes might make us happier!

3.4 Treatments for mood disorders

The biological approach: biochemistry

The brain produces chemicals to pass messages between different parts of the brain and the nervous system. These are known as neurotransmitters (because they transmit messages between neurons) and are proposed as a possible cause of depression. The amount of certain neurotransmitters in the brain may be reduced during depressive episodes and increased during periods of mania. Two neurotransmitters implicated in mood disorders are **noradrenaline** and serotonin.

The brain deactivates the neurotransmitter substance, once it has passed on the neural message, in two ways: either an enzyme (**monoamine oxidase**) is produced, which breaks down the chemical messenger (the neurons then have to produce more substances ready for the next firing) or the neurotransmitter is reabsorbed into the neuron that produced it. This process is known as **reuptake**. If reuptake does not occur, more substances must be produced.

Study 3.2

AIM Support for the biochemical approach was provided by Teuting *et al.* (1981).

METHOD A compound, produced when noradrenaline and serotonin are broken down by enzymes, is present in urine. Teuting analysed and compared urine samples from depressed and non-depressed participants.

RESULT Depressed patients' urine had lower than normal levels of the compounds.

CONCLUSION This suggested that depressed people have lower than normal activity of the neurotransmitters in the brain, which causes the depressed mood.

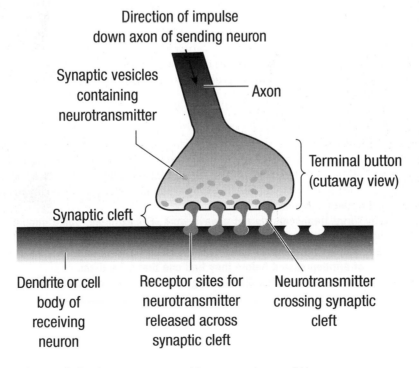

Figure 3.5: A neuron secreting neurotransmitters

EVALUATIVE COMMENT

One difficulty with the biological approach is whether we can establish causality. Do lower levels of neurotransmitters cause depression, or does depression cause a reduction in neurotransmitters?

The approach focuses largely on internal, physiological factors. However, depression may be a reaction to external life events, such as bereavement.

BIOCHEMICAL TREATMENT

One of the main advantages of the biochemical explanation is that it has enabled researchers to develop successful **psychotropic drug** treatments for mood disorders. These drugs are specifically designed to affect mental symptoms. Antidepressants are frequently used in the treatment of moderate to severe unipolar depression.

Early treatments known as tryclic antidepressants were discovered in 1958. These drugs prevent the reuptake of noradrenaline and serotonin, causing an increase of these substances in the brain. They were seen as a major breakthrough in the treatment of mood disorders because they reduced the number of hospital admissions, allowing people to visit their own GP and self-medicate.

Another class of antidepressants are the monoamine oxidase inhibitors (MAOIs). The drug works by stopping monoamine oxidase so that the levels of serotonin and noradrenaline in the brain increase. MAOIs seem to work better for some people than trycyclics.

A third and more recent class of antidepressant has been developed, known as selective serotonin reuptake inhibitors (SSRIs). As their name suggests, they selectively target serotonin, by stopping the reuptake process, thus increasing levels of serotonin in the brain. A well-known SSRI is called fluoxetine (Prozac).

Antidepressant drugs can be effective in the treatment of unipolar depression caused by low levels of certain neurotransmitters. However, in bipolar depression, it is likely that during the manic phase, the mood change is caused by an increase in levels of biochemicals. In 1949, it was discovered that a simple chemical compound, called lithium carbonate, could control the major mood swings of bipolar depression. Lithium occurs naturally in small proportions in much of our food. While scientists are not yet certain how the drug works, it is thought that it acts by affecting another neurochemical, which can either increase or decrease neural activity (Davison and Neale, 2001).

EVALUATIVE COMMENT

All antidepressants take some time to work. Interestingly, the increase in neurotransmitter substances occurs as soon as the patient begins to take the drug, but the effects are not felt immediately. Stirling and Hellewell (1999) argue that the drugs work not by increasing the amount of the neurotransmitter, but because they eventually alter the sensitivity of the receiving neurons, making them more effective.

Additionally, drug treatments do not always work. For example, some people with bipolar disorder report no change in manic episodes whilst taking lithium carbonate. In unipolar disorder, there can be variance in individual tolerance. The patient may have to try lots of different types of antidepressant before they find one that suits them.

Drug treatments have an added disadvantage because they can produce side effects (see Figure 3.6).

Type of drug	Possible side effects
Trycyclic antidepressants	A dry mouth, blurred vision
Monoamine oxidase inhibitors	Reaction with certain foods can cause increased blood pressure and heart failure, e.g. cheese, red wine
Selective serotonin reuptake inhibitors (SSRIs)	Fewer side effects for most people but when they occur they are more severe, including anxiety, hand tremors, upset stomach and insomnia
Lithium carbonate	Hand tremors, muscle twitching, blurred vision and confusion; prolonged use affects the kidney and liver functions

Figure 3.6: Side effects of drug treatments for depression

PRACTICAL Activity

Social factors may be implicated in the onset of depression. List ten possible social occurrences which might cause depression – for example, losing your job. Do you think that antidepressants should be prescribed for any of the social difficulties you have identified? What other suggestions can you make to reduce depression? Do these suggestions have any disadvantages?

GENETICS

Whilst there is little evidence of genetic factors in unipolar depression, research shows that bipolar depression runs in families. To ensure that the cause is biological, rather than learned behaviour, researchers have concentrated on an unusual group of people.

Study 3.3

AIM Price (1968) wanted to provide evidence of a genetic cause for bipolar depression.

METHOD He looked at sets of identical (monozygotic, or MZ) and non-identical (dizygotic, or DZ) twins. As the identical twins shared 100 per cent of their genes it was expected that they would have very similar psychological functioning. This similarity is called a concordance rate. There should be a lower concordance rate for DZ twins as they only share, on average, 50 per cent of their genes.

RESULT Price looked at 97 pairs of MZ twins who had been raised in the same family and found a concordance rate for bipolar disorder of 68 per cent. The concordance rate for MZ twins who had been raised apart (12 pairs) was almost the same (67 per cent). In 119 pairs of DZ twins, as expected, the concordance rate for bipolar disorder was lower at 23 per cent.

CONCLUSION This shows that biology and not other social factors, like being raised with an identical sibling, is a major contributory factor in bipolar depression.

EVALUATIVE COMMENT

While Price's study does provide evidence that genetic factors are important, if it were a wholly genetic disorder the concordance rate for MZ twins should be 100 per cent and for DZ twins 50 per cent. Other factors must be involved, to make the affected twin more vulnerable, or to protect the non-affected twin.

There have been fewer studies exploring the genetic contribution in unipolar disorder. Most research suggests that other social factors, such as unemployment, divorce or caring for small children in difficult circumstances, may be more important (Brown and Harris, 1978). These factors may also explain how some people appear to have a genetic predisposition (inherited tendency) to bipolar disorder, but do not develop it.

While research into the role of genes is ongoing, the approach does not as yet provide a method of treatment.

Psychodynamic approach

Freud (1917) thought that the symptoms of depression were very like grief. Mood disorders could be traced back to early childhood, when the personality was being formed. If the child experienced some form of loss (real or imagined) during these years, he or she would experience feelings of desertion and rejection when faced with loss in adult life. This re-experiencing of childhood is known as regression.

The relationship with parents, during early childhood, can cause the child to feel hostile towards them. Even the very best parents can not satisfy the needs of a demanding youngster all the time. These feelings would cause conflict within the child. To overcome this, anger is directed towards the self. This self-directed aggression creates feelings of despair and guilt.

Freud put forward a theory of personality suggesting that it consisted of three conflicting parts (see Chapter 1 of *Introducing Psychology*). The id (which you are born with) is greedy and unsocialised. The ego is the public part of the personality and develops when you are a toddler. The superego is the third and final aspect of the personality to emerge. It provides our moral code, or conscience. Freud thought that throughout life, the id and superego were in conflict. The ego attempts to maintain balance. Freud suggested that the symptoms of what we now call bipolar disorder can be explained by the interaction between parts of the personality. During the depressive stage, the superego gains control, making the individual feel guilty and worthless. The ego tries to assert itself and gain supremacy. This is what causes the manic phase. Eventually the superego takes over again and the individual is thrown back into depression.

EVALUATIVE COMMENT

Many critics point to the lack of scientific evidence for the psychodynamic approach. In terms of depression, some research indicates that early loss can contribute to depression in women. Brown and Harris (1978) undertook a survey of housewives in Camberwell, London. (See Study 1.5, page 19.) They found one factor that might make a person more vulnerable to depression was the early loss of a mother. However, this was only one of a number of vulnerability factors identified. Other problems, such as lack of employment, or having two or more children under the age of five, also had an effect. The impact of early loss may have more of an indirect influence.

Davison and Neale (1990) found no direct evidence that depressed people interpret the loss of a loved one as desertion or rejection. Most of us will have experienced some form of loss in childhood and yet we do not experience mood disorders later in life. However, the impact of a very traumatic childhood is acknowledged as one of the possible causes of psychological difficulties in adult life.

PSYCHODYNAMIC TREATMENTS

Freud was one of the first practitioners to suggest the 'talking cure', which he called psychoanalysis. The aim of the treatment is to help the patient (or client) to gain insight into their repressed conflicts, hidden in the unconscious mind. Freud believed this could be achieved by using a technique called free association. The client is asked to talk about anything that comes into their mind, without editing or censoring it. This can be quite difficult to do, because in everyday conversations we are constantly monitoring what we say, making sure it makes sense and checking for irrelevant ideas. With practice and encouragement from the therapist, however, free association should become easier. Freud thought that unconscious wishes and desires would eventually be revealed.

In addition, Freud also analysed the content of the client's dreams and their behaviour towards the therapist, to uncover unconscious conflicts from childhood. The role of the therapist was to interpret information gathered from the client, to help them gain insight into the cause of their depression. Freud believed that this would enable the client to have greater control over their emotions and reduce the likelihood of depressive symptoms.

Since Freud's time, a number of different talking cures, or psychotherapies, have been developed. For example, Klerman *et al.* (1984) concentrate more on the client's social interactions than on unconscious motivation.

EVALUATIVE COMMENT

Critics have pointed out that psychoanalysis is often lengthy, intensive and expensive. The treatment is therefore most successful with individuals who are highly motivated to solve their problems, who can verbalise their feelings easily, and have both the time and the money to undertake it (Davison and Neale, 2001). It is unlikely to be effective for bipolar disorder, because during the manic phase, the patient is unaware that their behaviour is disturbed.

The American Psychiatric Association (APA) conducted a review of studies in 1993 and concluded there had been no controlled data to support the effectiveness of long-term psychoanalysis in treating depression. However, other research – for example, that of Elkin (1989) – suggests that psychotherapy that focuses on improving the client's social relationships has helped to alleviate symptoms and reduce the likelihood of relapse.

PRACTICAL Activity

Research (Sloane *et al.*, 1975) has shown that the personal qualities of a therapist may have an impact on how successful the therapy is. Draw up a list of qualities that may have an effect. Give reasons for your choices. For example, age might be important. Clients might feel more comfortable with a counsellor who is slightly older than them. They may feel uncomfortable talking about their difficulties to a much younger or older person

Often clients have no control over who their counsellor is. They are sent to an available therapist, through the NHS. What effect (if any) will this have on the success of their therapy?

The behavioural approach

Behaviourists stress the importance of classical and operant conditioning. (You should remember these terms from your AS studies; see Chapter 1 of *Introducing Psychology*.)

Study 3.4

AIM Seligman (1974) focused on the process of classical conditioning. He undertook some research with dogs to show the importance of the environment in creating behaviour.

METHOD He gave the dogs painful electric shocks that they were unable to escape from. At first the dogs tried to get away from the shocks. Eventually they appeared to give up and simply accepted the situation. They were then placed in an environment where it was possible to escape from the shocks. They made no attempt to do so.

RESULT Seligman thought that the dogs were displaying **learned helplessness**. An unpleasant experience had taught them to remain passive and not take action.

CONCLUSION This led Seligman to believe that depression is a form of learned helplessness. People who have experienced failure could develop a sense of helplessness, leading to a mood disorder.

A second behavioural explanation was given by Lewinsohn (1974). He focused on the process of operant conditioning. He suggested that losing a loved one reduces the amount of positive reinforcement available to us. People who care about us will make us feel good about ourselves. If we have less opportunity to enjoy pleasant, rewarding experiences this may explain why we feel depressed. A depressed person will tend to withdraw socially and this will also reduce the likelihood of positive reinforcement. At first, the mood disorder may lead to concern from others. This attention also reinforces depressed behaviour. After a while, however, concern can fade away, adding to feelings of despair.

EVALUATIVE COMMENT

Seligman's work used animals and although he did undertake work with human participants, further studies have been unable to replicate his findings. After all, humans have a saying: 'If at first you don't succeed, try, try, try again.' There are also obvious ethical difficulties involved in these kinds of studies, where both animals and humans have been subjected to stressful situations.

While learned helplessness explains how life events cause unipolar depression, it does not really provide an explanation for the mood swings seen in bipolar disorder.

Also, Lewinsohn's theory can't explain why people don't recover from depression when they are no longer reinforced for it.

BEHAVIOURIST TREATMENTS

Behaviourist treatments are much less concerned with the underlying causes of the disorder than the psychodynamic treatments, concentrating instead on helping the person change what they do.

Sometimes failure can make us more determined to succeed: In the left hand photograph, David Beckham is sent off against Argentina during World Cup '98. On the right he scores the opening goal against Argentina during World Cup 2002.

Systematic desensitisation

The client must learn new behaviours to help them recover. For example, a person suffering from depression will often avoid social situations and feel anxious about communicating with others. According to the learned helplessness theory, this may be because they have previously had a bad experience in a social situation (for example, feeling embarrassed because they got a question wrong in class). Rather than facing the possibility of failing again, they withdraw from social contact and fall into depression. Systematic desensitisation aims to teach the person new strategies to help them relax, overcome their fears and change their behaviour.

The client would work with the therapist to draw up a hierarchy of anxiety-provoking events. This is a list of situations ranked from most difficult to cope with, down to least difficult. For example, answering a question in a classroom could provoke maximum anxiety, speaking to the bus driver on the way to college might be perceived as less stressful.

The client is then asked to imagine being in these situations, starting with the least stressful. If they experience any anxiety during this process, they are asked to use their newly developed relaxation techniques. The approach works through classical conditioning. The client is learning to associate a new response with a previously distressing stimulus. Eventually the client will be asked to experience the situations in real life. A change in the client's behaviour should lead to a reduction in the symptoms of depression.

Positive reinforcement

The client is asked to perform certain tasks to increase the likelihood of social interaction. The therapist will monitor and praise the individual for changing their behaviour. The approach works through a process of operant conditioning. Members of the client's family may be asked to ignore any depressive symptoms shown and praise positive action.

EVALUATIVE COMMENT

Behaviour therapy can be very useful in treating anxiety, but this is only one of the possible symptoms of depression. The client must be highly motivated to change and prepared to experience stressful situations. Many depressed people would find the regime too difficult to maintain and, again, it is not particularly effective in controlling manic episodes.

The approach doesn't look for underlying causes and tends to focus on behaviour rather than thoughts and feelings. However, it has been successfully combined with cognitive approaches to create a new treatment method called cognitive behaviour therapy (CBT).

PRACTICAL Activity

Draw up a list of ten activities to increase a client's social interaction. For example, a relatively easy activity could be asking them to go into a shop, buy a newspaper and comment on the weather to the shop assistant. Put these activities into a hierarchy, from most difficult to least difficult. Can you think of any problems in asking a client to do these things? What would the therapist do if a client failed in any of the tasks?

The cognitive approach

The cognitive theory of depression suggests that people become depressed because they tend to think in self-defeating ways. Beck (1987) proposed that people develop 'schemas' during childhood and adolescence. Schemas are the mental rules that govern the way we see the world. They guide our behaviour. For example, you will have a mental rule about the use of drugs that will affect whether you are tempted to try them or not. According to Beck, people who become depressed have developed **negative schemas**. They have a tendency to view themself, the world and the future in pessimistic ways.

A person might develop negative schemas as a result of bad experiences with parents, other family members, authority figures or peers. Four different types of negative thinking can be seen in Figure 3.8.

Arbitrary inference	Drawing negative conclusions about oneself with insufficient evidence, e.g. It rained on my birthday so I must be useless.
Selective abstraction	Focusing on one negative aspect of a situation and ignoring others, e.g. My team lost the match because only I played badly.
Overgeneralisation	Making a sweeping conclusion on the basis of one event, e.g. I am a complete failure because I failed a surprise test in class.
Magnification and minimisation	Tending to magnify failure and minimise success, e.g. I am hideously ugly because I have a tiny skin blemish. I passed the test because it was really easy.

Figure 3.8: Types of negative thinking

Study 3.5

AIM Weissman and Beck (1978) investigated the thought processes of depressed people to establish if they were using negative schemas.

METHOD Thought processes were measured using the dysfunctional attitude scale (DAS). Participants were asked to fill in a questionnaire by ticking whether they agreed or disagreed with a set of statements. For example, 'People will probably think less of me if I make a mistake.'

RESULT Beck found that depressed participants made more negative assessments than non-depressed people. When given some therapy to challenge and change their negative schemas there was an improvement in their self-ratings.

CONCLUSION Depression involves the use of negative schemas.

EVALUATIVE COMMENT

One difficulty with this approach is whether psychologists can establish causality. Do the negative thoughts cause depression, or does depression cause negative thoughts?

Also, the DAS questionnaire lacks 'ecological validity': it is measuring responses to hypothetical statements rather than assessing actual events and thoughts. (You may remember from your AS-level work some of the problems of using questionnaires.) However, Beck's ideas have been applied in the real world. Cognitive therapy has been shown to be effective in the treatment of some mood and anxiety disorders.

COGNITIVE TREATMENTS

Beck (1976) developed a therapy to challenge the negative schemas of the client. First, the client will be assessed to discover the severity of their condition. The therapist will establish a baseline (or starting point), prior to treatment, to help monitor improvement.

The therapist must make the client aware of the relationship between thought and emotion. For example, if you think you are stupid, it may make you feel sad. If you feel sad, you will not enjoy what you are doing. Thoughts influence emotions and behaviour. To feel better you must think positively. The client is asked to provide information about how they perceive themselves, the future and the world. The therapist would use a process of reality testing. For example, if the client says 'I'm useless, I always fail', they will be asked whether, in reality, they have been successful at something. The client's beliefs are directly challenged and they are made aware of their negative views. The therapist may ask the client to do something to demonstrate their ability to succeed. In this way, irrational ideas can be replaced with more optimistic and rational beliefs.

EVALUATIVE COMMENT

Cognitive therapy has been very successful in treating unipolar depression. However, the client must be motivated and committed to change. Some people may find the approach too directive and confrontational.

Beck acknowledged, that as well as changing negative thoughts, the client must also be encouraged to alter their behaviour. He would set clients homework, or 'activity assignments'. Clients are encouraged to interact with others, to help them feel good about themselves. This combination approach is called cognitive behaviour therapy.

Approach	Cause	Treatment method	Good points	Bad points
Biological	Neurochemistry or genetics	Antidepressant drugs	Quick, effective treatment	Side effects, treats symptoms only
Psychodynamic				
Behavioural				
Cognitive				

Figure 3.9: Summary of the main approaches to mood disorders

PRACTICAL Activity

Summarise the main approaches to SAD, unipolar and bipolar depression. Use Figure 3.9 to help you.

Effectiveness of treatments

There are many different treatment methods available for mental health problems; each has limitations, however. The effectiveness of the treatment may depend on the psychological attributes of the patient (see Chapter 4). For example, a motivated person, who likes to think their way through problems, may benefit from the cognitive approach. Mohr (1995) looked at a group of patients whose therapy had been unsuccessful. He found that patients who were poorly motivated, who thought that therapy would be easy, or who had poor interpersonal skills, were most likely to report negative outcomes.

A second factor we have already identified (see Practical Activity, page 65) is the client/therapist relationship.

Study 3.6

AIM Sloane *et al.* (1975) wanted to identify the main factors contributing to recovery from depression.

METHOD He conducted a study on two groups of patients who had benefited from either behavioural or psychodynamic therapy. Each group was asked to identify the main factors contributing to their recovery.

RESULT Both groups reported being able to talk to a sympathetic and encouraging person as an important part of their therapy.

CONCLUSION The personality of the therapist may be as crucial as the type of therapy given.

Drug treatments are not dependent on the strength of a therapeutic relationship. Also, patients do not have to feel personally responsible for a chemical imbalance taking place within the body. Consequently, some patients may be better suited to this form of treatment.

Stirling and Hellewell (1999) suggest that the severity of the depression should be taken into account when assessing which treatment to offer. Therapy may be useful for patients with less severe or persistent depressive states. For long-term, clinical depression (such as bipolar depression) it is likely to be less effective than drug treatments.

Establishing which treatment is the most effective is as problematic as trying to identify a single cause for depression. Humans are complex and the way forward may be a combination of the current treatments available.

3.5 Schizophrenia

Schizophrenia is not, as many people think, a split personality. The 'split' in schizophrenia occurs between the person's thought processes and reality. It is categorised as a psychosis and affects one in one hundred people, with equal numbers of males and females. Before the 1950s, many people with schizophrenia spent most of their lives in psychiatric hospitals. This is known as institutionalisation. New treatment methods have changed this. About 25 per cent of sufferers will get better after only one episode of the illness, 50–65 per cent will improve, but continue to have bouts of the illness. The remainder will have persistent difficulties (Stirling and Hellewell, 1999).

Classification

There are four main types of schizophrenic disorder: disorganised, catatonic, paranoid and undifferentiated. Each of these is described briefly below.

DISORGANISED SCHIZOPHRENIA

Symptoms include thought disturbances, an absence of expressed emotion and a loss of interest in life. The person's behaviour is generally disorganised and not goal directed.

CATATONIC SCHIZOPHRENIA

Catatonic schizophrenia is diagnosed if the patient has severe motor abnormalities such as unusual gestures or use of body language. Sometimes patients gesture repeatedly, using complex sequences of finger, hand and arm movements, which appear to have some meaning to them.

PARANOID SCHIZOPHRENIA

Delusional symptoms and hallucinations are present; however, the patient remains emotionally responsive. They are more alert and verbal than patients with other types of schizophrenia.

UNDIFFERENTIATED SCHIZOPHRENIA

This type is diagnosed when the patient shows symptoms of schizophrenia but does not fit into the three other types.

Symptoms and diagnosis of schizophrenia

Schizophrenia is a psychosis that is categorised in both the *DSM* and *ICD* (see Chapter 1). The symptoms are divided into two groups. Some symptoms are rare in normal, everyday experiences; these are known as **positive symptoms**. Other symptoms are much less dramatic and can be experienced in everyday life; these are known as **negative symptoms**. A person may also be affected by **secondary symptoms** such as depression, as a result of the difficulties of living with the disorder (Davison and Neale, 2001).

POSITIVE SYMPTOMS

Hallucinations

The most common hallucination is an experience of 'hearing voices'. People with schizophrenia can hear their own thoughts, but also report other inner voices. The voices may appear to talk to each other, as well as talking to them. The thoughts can be so loud that the sufferer believes other people nearby can also hear them. This is known as thought broadcasting. The voices may appear to come from outside – for example, from the television. Visions and hallucinations of smell, taste or being touched can also occur, although they are less common.

Delusions

A delusion is a particular kind of unusual belief, which is experienced without any evidence to support it. Some sufferers experience paranoid delusions where they believe that others are trying to harm them. Others have delusions of reference. This is where you start to see special meanings in ordinary events. For example, you may believe that a radio programme is specifically about you. Grandiose delusions are where the sufferer has an exaggerated sense of power, knowledge or identity – for example, believing that they can save the world.

Thought disturbances

A person with a thought disturbance may appear incoherent. It is difficult to understand what they are talking about, because they seem to jump from one topic to the next. There can also be a lack of concentration. Some people describe their thoughts as 'misty' or 'hazy'. They cannot remember what it is they want to say or do.

NEGATIVE SYMPTOMS

There may be a lack of energy, and a loss of interest in life. It can be difficult to wash or tidy up, or to keep clean. This is known as **avolition**. The person may also stop showing any emotion and appear lifeless. They may stare vacantly and speak in a flat, toneless voice. This is called **flat affect**. While the negative symptoms are much less dramatic, they tend to last for longer than the positive symptoms. Ho *et al.* (1998) found that the presence of many negative symptoms is a strong predictor of a poor quality of life, two years after the initial diagnosis.

SECONDARY SYMPTOMS

These symptoms are thought to result from the consequences of having the disorder. Some sufferers report depression, or an inability to maintain existing relationships or make new friends. It may be difficult to find and keep employment. The extent to which somebody is

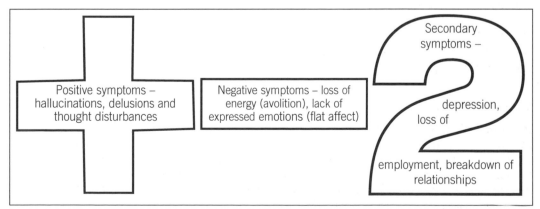

Figure 3.10: Summary of the positive, negative and secondary symptoms of schizophrenia

affected by secondary symptoms may depend on their support systems, how quickly they were diagnosed and how effective their treatment is.

DIAGNOSIS

In Britain, one or more positive symptoms must be present for a diagnosis to be made (Stirling and Hellewell, 1999). Alternatively, two negative symptoms may also lead to a diagnosis. The symptoms must have been apparent for at least one month. The illness usually occurs gradually and has three phases (see Figure 3.11).

Schizophrenia rarely starts before the age of 15, and although it affects men and women equally, there are differences in the age of onset. Men usually notice symptoms in their late teens or early twenties. Women are often affected later, in their twenties and thirties.

Someone with schizophrenia may not realise they are ill and can refuse treatment when they need it. As a result they can be admitted to hospital against their will under the Mental Health Act. This should only happen if their health is at risk, if they are a danger to themselves, or if they may be a danger to others (see Chapter 4).

The **prodomal** (first) phase	The individual becomes withdrawn and loses interest in work, school and leisure activities
The **active** phase	More obvious positive symptoms begin to occur; the duration of this phase can vary; for some people it lasts a few months, whereas others remain in the active phase
The **residual** phase	The obvious symptoms begin to subside

Figure 3.11: The phases of schizophrenia

EVALUATIVE COMMENT

There are many different symptoms and types of this disorder. Two people may be diagnosed and yet have completely different characteristics.

Romme and Escher (2000) claimed that 'hearing voices' is not necessarily indicative of a psychotic illness. They surveyed 15000 non-schizophrenic people and found that between 10 and 15 per cent had experienced voice-hearing, often the voice of a loved one after bereavement.

PRACTICAL Activity

Draw two circles on a large piece of paper so that they intersect each other at one point. Write the symptoms of bipolar disorder and schizophrenia in these circles, putting symptoms present in more than one disorder in the intersecting area. Do you think psychiatrists may have difficulty in diagnosing which disorder the patient has? What is the key difference?

3.6 Explanations and treatments for schizophrenia

The biological approach

GENETICS

Like unipolar disorder, research has focused on twin studies. Gottesman and Shields (1972) found that the concordance rate for schizophrenia in MZ twins was 48 per cent compared to a 10 per cent rate for DZ twins.

Study 3.7

AIM Heston (1966) investigated the role of genetics in schizophrenia.

METHOD He compared 47 adopted children whose biological mother had schizophrenia with a control group of adopted children with no history of schizophrenia in their biological family.

RESULT None of the controls was diagnosed with the illness; 16 per cent of the offspring of schizophrenic mothers were diagnosed.

CONCLUSION This indicated that inheritance does play a part in the disorder.

EVALUATIVE COMMENT

These studies show that the cause of the illness is not wholly genetic, and indicate an inherited predisposition. The diathesis stress model of mental illness suggests that inheritance can put people at risk; however, stress may also play a part.

It has also not been possible to identify whether a single gene or several genes are implicated or how they influence the emergence of symptoms. Research in this area continues but as yet offers no method of treatment.

REFLECTIVE Activity

Researchers have not yet been able to pinpoint what kinds of external events may trigger the disorder. For example, exam stress may be one reason why schizophrenia occurs in men in their late teens. Think of another event and outline the research method you would use to investigate it. Are there any ethical difficulties with this kind of research?

BIOCHEMICAL EXPLANATIONS

An excess of the neurotransmitter **dopamine** has been implicated in schizophrenia (Davison and Neale, 2001). Dopamine is a substance that is known to be active in the limbic system, an area of the brain governing emotion. Evidence to support the dopamine hypothesis comes from the following sources:

- The effects of drugs used to treat patients with Parkinson's disease. This degenerative brain disease is known to be caused by a decrease in dopamine. Drug treatments to increase dopamine levels in Parkinson's patients can have side effects similar to the symptoms of schizophrenia.

- Antipsychotic drugs, which reduce the levels of dopamine, are effective in reducing the symptoms of schizophrenia (Kimble, 1988).

- Post-mortems conducted on schizophrenic patients show high levels of dopamine in the brain (Iversen, 1979).

- Amphetamines and cocaine increase dopamine levels. Some drug users experience schizophrenia-like symptoms (Davis, 1974).

EVALUATIVE COMMENT

Again, there are problems in establishing causality. Does excess dopamine cause schizophrenia, or does the illness have an effect on dopamine levels? Like bipolar depression, it may be that receptors in the brain of a person with schizophrenia are more sensitive, rather than the level of neurotransmitter (Stirling and Hellewell, 1999).

Further biological research has concentrated less on biochemical effects and more on possible structural abnormalities in the brain. Stevens (1982) showed that there are differences in eye movement with schizophrenic patients. These kinds of differences are usually seen in patients with brain damage.

ANTIPSYCHOTIC DRUG TREATMENTS

The most important development in the treatment of schizophrenia has been the introduction of **antipsychotic drugs**. These drugs can reduce the positive symptoms of psychosis. In 1954 a drug called chlorpromazine was introduced. It blocks dopamine receptors in the brain. This means that neurons do not respond to dopamine. The drugs usually weaken positive symptoms gradually over a few weeks, and thought processes become clearer. However, side effects can occur, including tremors, drowsiness and weight gain. About one in twenty people experience permanent movements in the tongue and mouth.

Newer drugs called atypical antipsychotics work on a wider range of neurotransmitters, including serotonin. They have fewer side effects and can help reduce negative symptoms.

Both types of drugs can be taken daily by mouth or by injection every three to four weeks.

EVALUATIVE COMMENT

Drug treatments were seen to be a major breakthrough in the treatment of schizophrenia. They have reduced the number of long-stay patients in hospitals and enabled sufferers to live in the community. However, some patients do not respond and find the side effects, such as tremors or drowsiness, difficult to cope with.

Also, drug treatments are not a cure. If the sufferer stops taking the medication, the symptoms can return.

Psychodynamic approach

Freud believed that schizophrenia emerged due to conflict between different parts of the personality. In adult schizophrenia, the ego is overwhelmed, by either the id or the superego. As a result the ego (or public part of the personality) regresses back to infancy. The individual has delusions of self-importance, very like the demanding and unsocialised behaviour of a baby. Fantasies become confused with reality, as the ego tries to get control. Hallucinations and delusions will then emerge, as the ego struggles to regain a sense of reality.

EVALUATIVE COMMENT

Unfortunately there is no scientific evidence to support Freud's ideas on schizophrenia. Stirling and Hellewell (1999) point out that schizophrenic behaviour is not similar to infantile behaviour. Research has not found a correlation between early childhood experiences and a subsequent diagnosis. However, the role of family members has been implicated in sociocultural explanations, as we will see later in this chapter.

PSYCHODYNAMIC TREATMENTS

Freud didn't use psychoanalysis with schizophrenic patients. He thought they were incapable of forming a close interpersonal relationship with the therapist and the technique would therefore fail. However, Sullivan (1929) pioneered the use of psychotherapy with hospitalised patients. He too believed that schizophrenia was a regressive process. The sufferer returns to a child-like state, because they experienced childhood trauma and are unable to handle the stresses of adult communication. Sullivan thought that a trusting relationship could be slowly built up with the patient, which would eventually lead to success. The therapist could help the patient to develop a stronger ego, by examining their relationships from the past.

EVALUATIVE COMMENT

Critics have pointed out that Sullivan's patients were only mildly disturbed and may not have been diagnosed with schizophrenia using current criteria.

A review of psychotherapy undertaken by Katz and Gunderson (1990) found that the technique may even prove harmful for patients with positive symptoms.

The behavioural approach

The behavioural approach explains schizophrenia as a learned response. Ullman and Krasner (1969) argue that people will behave in a schizophrenic way if they are reinforced for it. The disorder develops through a process of operant conditioning. Bizarre behaviour gains attention from other people, so may be reinforced more than normal behaviour. Through a process of social learning, patients in hospitals may also observe and imitate the behaviour of other schizophrenics (see Chapter 4 of *Introducing Psychology*).

EVALUATIVE COMMENT

This approach does not really explain how schizophrenic symptoms emerge in the first place – for example, why a person would report hearing voices rather than adopting any other kind of behaviour. Critics argue that it oversimplifies a complex and distressing condition by reducing it to an attention-seeking strategy.

However, social learning theory can be used to explain how patients' symptoms can multiply after diagnosis, because hospitalisation increases the amount of social contact with other patients displaying unusual behaviour.

BEHAVIOURAL TREATMENTS

Study 3.8

AIM Paul and Lentz (1977) investigated the effectiveness of operant conditioning by reinforcing appropriate behaviour with schizophrenic patients.

METHOD They set up a token economy system in a hospital ward. The patients were given tokens as a reward each time they behaved appropriately. These could be used to purchase meals and small luxury items. For example, making your bed earned a token. Patients also received individual behavioural treatments tailored to their own needs. Their progress was followed up every six months, for a period of six years, by interview and direct observation.

RESULT Paul and Lentz found that both positive and negative symptoms were significantly reduced, leading to more hospital discharges when compared to a control group. The research also found that only 11 per cent of patients continued to need drug treatment, compared to 100 per cent of the control group.

CONCLUSION Operant conditioning is an effective means of treating people with chronic schizophrenia.

EVALUATIVE COMMENT

While this is a very impressive study, Paul (1981) later concluded that the token economy was useful mainly in gaining the attention of the patients. However, the most important factor in their recovery was the social skills training given by the staff. The training is used to teach people the right way to behave in a wide variety of social situations. Patients are helped through role play, tuition and experience to develop new skills and consolidate existing ones.

The cognitive approach

Schizophrenia is characterised by disturbance in language, attention, thought and perception. This has led cognitive psychologists to explain it as a result of faulty information processing.

We are constantly bombarded with information from the outside world yet our information-processing abilities are limited. As a result, the brain selects which information to pay attention to, and ignores the rest. Auditory selective attention is the process by which the brain selects which sounds to respond to. Pickering (1981) proposed that catatonic schizophrenia may be caused by a breakdown in auditory selective attention, making social interaction increasingly difficult, as the individual is overloaded with auditory information. Pickering believes that withdrawal from the world is the only way for catatonic schizophrenics to keep sensory stimulation at a manageable level.

Frith (1992) suggested that schizophrenics fail to monitor their own thoughts, misattributing them to the outside world. When a person hears voices, it is actually their own inner speech being misinterpreted.

EVALUATIVE COMMENT

The cognitive approach explains how information processing is affected in schizophrenia but does not provide an explanation of what causes these cognitive changes. The disorder is typically diagnosed in adulthood and, as yet, there is no scientific evidence to link childhood difficulties in information processing with later onset of schizophrenia.

However, the approach is currently being used to develop new strategies of coping with the disorder and research in this area is ongoing.

COGNITIVE TREATMENT

This is a relatively new development in the treatment of schizophrenia and has caused some controversy. Some practitioners believe that voice-hearers can be helped to bring the voices under their control, using cognitive behavioural techniques. The idea has led to a renewed interest in the role of psychotherapy, however the emphasis is on controlling thought processes rather than uncovering unconscious wishes (Bentall *et al.*, 1994). The process begins by asking the patient to focus on the nature of the voices they hear – for example, thinking about their tone, or whether they are male or female. They might also find external ways of focusing, by drawing pictures of the different voices. Therapists help the patient to recognise that the voices represent part of their own thought processes. An 'evil' voice may represent their own desire for self-harm. Patients are also encouraged to develop strategies to protect them against the wishes of these inner voices. For example, relaxation techniques, talking to supportive others, or only choosing to pay attention at a certain time of day.

EVALUATIVE COMMENT

Many psychiatrists are concerned that the approach may encourage and support delusional thinking in their patients. Paying attention to the content of voices may result in the client doing what the voice instructs, rather than controlling it. However, Romme and Escher (2000) disagree, claiming that focusing on voices actually reduces the likelihood of harm to the self or others.

PRACTICAL Activity

You can experience the effect of voice-hearing on your thoughts, feelings and behaviour. Try having a conversation with a friend, while another friend sits by your shoulder and talks quietly about something else in your ear. How easy is it to continue? What effect does it have on your ability to concentrate? How do you feel? Look back at some of the symptoms of schizophrenia. Could some of the positive or negative symptoms be explained as the consequences of voice-hearing?

Sociocultural explanations

LABELLING

Szasz (1962) claims that schizophrenia does not exist. He believes it is a way of classifying people whose behaviour is bizarre and difficult to control. 'Mental illness' is simply a label used to exclude people who don't conform.

Scheff (1966) argued that receiving a psychiatric diagnosis creates a stigma or mark of social disgrace. The label 'mental illness' creates expectations from the patient and others. As a result the behaviour of the patient may change towards those expectations. The diagnosis thus creates a 'self-fulfilling prophecy'.

Study 3.9

AIM Rosenhan (1973) provided a powerful example of the effect of labelling.

METHOD He asked eight psychologically healthy people to arrange appointments at different hospitals. They were to complain that they could hear a voice in their head, which said words like 'thud' and 'hollow'. All eight pseudo-patients were admitted to hospital; seven were diagnosed with schizophrenia. Rosenhan instructed the participants to act normally once they were in hospital, not to take any medication given and to try to convince staff that they were sane. They were also asked to observe and record their experiences on the ward.

RESULT The pseudo-patients were kept on the ward for an average of 19 days. The longest stay was 52 days. All but one of the participants were released with a diagnosis of 'schizophrenia in remission'. None of them managed to convince medical staff that they were sane. The pseudo-patients observed how normal behaviour was viewed as 'schizophrenic'. For example, queuing for lunch was described by one psychiatrist as 'oral acquisitive syndrome'. The participants were often ignored by staff, creating a sense of powerlessness and fear. Other patients did recognise 'normality' and asked the pseudo-patients if they were reporters!

CONCLUSION Perceptions of patients are affected by the labels they have been given.

EVALUATIVE COMMENT

This study contributed to a revision of methods for diagnosis and patient care. It also contributed to the debate surrounding institutionalisation, which we will consider at the end of the chapter. However, there are ethical problems, as deception was involved.

Labelling theory has provoked many practitioners to re-examine their own expectations. Even so, distressed, disoriented and deluded people, with a range of symptoms, do exist and require help. The theory does not provide any viable means of treatment for these people.

PRACTICAL Activity

Look through newspapers to find articles featuring schizophrenia. Do they provide information and advice or are they 'labelling'? Is there any difference in the way the illness is portrayed in tabloids (like the *Sun*) compared to broadsheet newspapers (like the *Guardian*)?

THE ONLY THING GREATER THAN THE POWER OF THE MIND
IS THE COURAGE OF THE HEART.

A FILM BY RON HOWARD

RUSSELL
CROWE A
BEAUTIFUL
MIND

Are media
images of
mental
health
problems
changing?

FAMILY DYSFUNCTION

The importance of family relationships has been put forward as a possible explanation for schizophrenia. The approach is sociocultural because it does not look to the individual sufferer. It concentrates on the social and cultural environment. Early theorists, influenced by Freudian ideas, thought that a 'schizogenic' mother, who was cold, dominant and created conflict, caused schizophrenia to emerge in the child. These mothers were said to be rejecting, overprotective, self-sacrificing, moralistic about sex and fearful of intimacy.

Bateson *et al.* (1956) thought that faulty communication within families was a possible cause. They called this the **double bind**. Parents place children in a 'no win' situation by giving them contradictory messages. For example, a father might ask for a hug and then push the child away, telling them they are too old for cuddles. This theory suggests that children will become confused and lose their grip on reality. They will begin to mistrust their own thoughts and feelings.

EVALUATIVE COMMENT

There is no clear evidence to support the claim that family relationships create schizophrenia. Klebanoff (1959) has argued that strained family communication may be the result of dealing with an already unusual child. However, some studies have indicated a family role in the recovery of already diagnosed schizophrenics.

Study 3.10

AIM Brown *et al.* (1966) investigated the impact of family relationships on the recovery of schizophrenic patients.

METHOD They conducted a nine-month follow-up of schizophrenic patients discharged from hospital. Interviews were conducted with family members. The conversations were rated for the number of critical comments or hostility towards the patient.

RESULT Brown *et al.* found that families who were high in expressed emotion (EE) were critical of the patient; 58 per cent of patients from high EE families returned to hospital for further treatment, compared to only 10 per cent of those from low expressed emotion families.

CONCLUSION Family relationships can affect the recovery rates of people with schizophrenia.

Effectiveness of treatment methods

At the moment the most effective treatment for schizophrenia is the use of antipsychotic drugs, although, as we have already noted, they can have unpleasant side effects for patients. Behavioural treatments have been successful in changing the behaviour of long-term schizophrenic patients but they do not remove cognitive symptoms, like voice-hearing or delusions. Traditional psychotherapy has been largely discounted as a treatment method, however researchers are investigating the effectiveness of more cognitive therapies. These techniques may be useful in providing coping strategies for patients, to successfully manage their symptoms and reduce the likelihood of relapse. Research (Bentall *et al.*, 1994) suggests that cognitive therapy may be most effective for patients experiencing their first episode of schizophrenia. All of these treatments focus solely on the individual and ignore the impact of their social and family situation. Mental health practitioners may need to broaden their focus to this wider community to find ways to improve recovery rates.

Institutional care and community care

Because there were no effective treatments available, until the 1960s many patients spent a very long time (in some instances 30 years or more) in state mental hospitals. While this meant that they were under medical supervision and being physically looked after, it also produced additional problems. For example, patients in hospitals can observe and imitate the behaviour of other schizophrenics. Also, the hospital ward provides little information about how to survive and fend for yourself in the outside world. This led to many patients becoming institutionalised. They did not have the necessary social skills to succeed outside the institution. With the advent of new drug treatments, the incidence of long-term care has been significantly reduced. Many mental hospitals have now been closed and replaced by community care programmes.

Community care aims to provide the patient with continued support outside the hospital ward. Psychiatric nurses visit patients at home to monitor them and help sort out problems with medication. Occupational therapists can give advice on building important social skills. The patient may attend hospital day clinics and see a clinical psychologist occasionally. They can also attend day centres within the community, where they can meet with other people. Some areas also have work projects to help people get back into employment. Patients may also be provided with supported accommodation where they have their own flat or bedsit, but a member of staff also lives on the premises.

Research has tried to evaluate the impact of community-based treatment programmes as compared with standard in-patient care, as shown in Study 3.11.

Study 3.11

AIM Stein and Test (1980) wanted to find out if community care was better than hospitalisation for people with schizophrenia.

METHOD They compared two groups of 65 patients. Participants in one group received standard in-patient treatment. The second group received a training programme to enable them to live in the community. The following aspects were examined:

- the availability of resources to the patients, such as food and shelter
- training in basic social and community skills
- reducing dependency on family or institutions
- support and education of key carers in the patient's life
- developing a social network.

RESULT During the first 12 months of the study, 58 of the in-patients had been re-admitted for further treatment, compared to only 12 of the patients who received the training. Unfortunately, when the training programme ended, many patients from the community care group were later re-admitted to hospital.

CONCLUSION Care in the community can be successful, provided patients are given constant support. However, community care is not a 'cure' and patients will continue to experience symptoms.

Shepherd (1998) has argued that community care can be successful if specialist teams – made up of psychologists, occupational therapists, social workers, psychiatrists and nurses – have small caseloads of 10 to 15 patients. Help should be made available for clients both day and night. Continuity of care workers is also important.

EVALUATIVE COMMENT

Critics of community care are concerned that there are differences in the quality of service provided across the country, depending on available funding in local areas. Some patients simply 'slip through the net' and do not receive the care and attention they need, with very negative consequences for the individual and others.

Institutionalisation does have some positive consequences. A controlled environment allows the close monitoring, support and treatment of those suffering with a mental illness. It can prevent harm to the self or others.

REFLECTIVE Activity

You should now have read enough to consider the implications of a diagnosis of schizophrenia. Look back to page 68 and the Study on page 76, and use Figure 3.14 as a template to help you summarise these.

Mental health	Treatment should reduce the number of symptoms experienced and help the individual to become more stable
Work or employment opportunities	
Relationships with family or friends	
Self-perception	
Physical health	

Figure 3.13: A summary of the implications of a diagnosis of schizophrenia

FINAL NOTE

This area of the specification can be useful to return to when you begin the 'Debates in Psychology' section of the course. For example, the biological approach adopts a *nature* argument to explain mood disorders and schizophrenia, whereas the behaviourist approach supports an *environmental* cause. Psychodynamic approaches are *idiographic,* whereas behaviourism or biological explanations adopt a *nomothetic* approach. The *mind and body* debate can also be considered by comparing the psychodynamic approach to the biological approach.

3.7 Sample questions

SAMPLE QUESTION

(a) Explain one consequence of being diagnosed with schizophrenia.

(AO1 = 1, AO2 = 2)   (3 marks)

(b) Distinguish between the positive and negative symptoms of schizophrenia.

(AO1 = 1, AO2 = 2)   (3 marks)

(c) Describe and evaluate the use of both psychotherapy and drug therapy in the treatment of schizophrenia.

(AO1 = 7, AO2 = 7)   (14 marks)

Total AO1 marks = 9   Total AO2 marks = 11   Total = 20 marks

QUESTIONS, ANSWERS AND COMMENTS

(a) John had been feeling intensely sad for a time and had gradually withdrawn from social activities. Most days he was tired and irritable. One morning he got up early and felt unusually energetic. He telephoned lots of people even though it was only 6 am and then went into town and bought a motorbike. He talked incessantly to anyone who would listen.

With reference to John's behaviour, explain whether he is displaying symptoms of unipolar or bipolar disorder.

(AO1 = 1, AO2 = 2)   (3 marks)

(b) Explain one consequence for John of being diagnosed as suffering from depression.

(AO1 = 1, AO2 = 2)   (3 marks)

(c) Describe and discuss one cognitive treatment for depression.

(AO1 = 7, AO2 = 7)   (14 marks)

Total AO1 marks = 9   Total AO2 marks = 11   Total = 20 marks

Answer to (a)

John is displaying symptoms of bipolar depression because he is irritable and not sleeping properly. These are symptoms of depression.

Comment: 1 mark (AO1) awarded for correctly identifying the depression; 1 mark (AO2) awarded for application of knowledge to the stimulus material. A further AO2 mark would have been given if the answer had identified a symptom of mania.

Answer to (b)

John may have to be placed under section of the Mental Health Act, which allows hospital treatment to be given without his consent.

Comment: 1 mark (AO1) awarded for identifying one consequence; no marks awarded for AO2 as there is no analysis of how the consequence might affect John – for example, how his life may become more stable and easier if he gets appropriate treatment.

Answer to (c)

Beck's cognitive therapy is one way of treating depression. He thought that faulty thinking was the main cause of depressive symptoms such as feeling unhappy and withdrawing from social contact. The cognitive approach believes that thoughts affect feelings and behaviour. In order to feel better and act differently the patient must be shown how to think in more positive ways. Beck believed there are several ways of thinking negatively, such as overgeneralisation and arbitrary influence. Overgeneralisation is where a person has experienced a failure in one part of their life and then generalises this sense of failure to all areas. For example, I missed the bus this morning so I must be completely stupid. Arbitrary inferences occur when a person makes negative assumptions about themselves based on irrational or illogical evidence. For example, it rained on my birthday so I must be a bad person.

These negative ways of thinking are inaccurate and must be challenged by the therapist. Beck would instruct the patient to act like a scientist, making more positive predictions about the future and then seeking evidence to support their hypothesis. For example, going out more often will make me feel better about myself. The patient is asked to gather information about success rather than focusing on bad thoughts and feelings. They are also encouraged to set goals that they think they can realistically reach. This will give the patient a sense of achievement. Every positive thought and action is praised by the therapist. In this way the cognitive approach also combines behavioural techniques, by using operant conditioning and positive reinforcement.

Research has shown that cognitive therapy can be very effective for treating depression. However, the patient must be very motivated to change, and this might be difficult for some people. Drug treatments for depression do not rely on motivation so some people might be prefer to take antidepressants instead. Also, it ignores unconscious motivation.

Comment: 5 marks (AO1) awarded for the description, which was clear and made reference to how therapy attempts to alter negative thoughts such as overgeneralisation. Reference to how progress is monitored would add marks here. 4 marks (AO2) awarded – the answer shows application of knowledge by giving examples of the theory. Some attempt at evaluation and reference to other approaches is made although this is rather limited.

Overall (for parts a, b and c) this answer would gain 12 out of 20 and is a good answer.

3.8 FURTHER READING

Introductory texts

Davison, G.C. & Neale, J.M. 2001: **Abnormal Psychology**. 8th Ed. Wiley, New York

Gross, R. & McIlveen, R. 2000: **Psychopathology**. Hodder & Stoughton, London

Stirling, J.D. & Hellewell, S.E. 1999: **Psychopathology. Atypical Development and Abnormal Behaviour**. Routledge, London and New York

Specialist sources

Brown, G.W. & Harris, T.O. 1978: **The Social Origins of Depression**. Tavistock, London

Torrey, E.F. 1988: **Surviving Schizophrenia**. Harper & Row, New York

Useful websites

www.mentalhealth.org.uk The Mental Health Foundation

www.sane.org.uk SANE

www.repych.ac.uk The Royal College of Psychiatrists

www.nsf.org.uk The National Schizophrenia Foundation

Sample questions, answers and comments

4 Treatment of atypical behaviour

4.1 Introduction

As we have seen in Chapters 2 and 3, people suffering from psychological disorders can exhibit a wide range of symptoms with differing levels of severity. For example, cognitive difficulties are apparent in depression, with symptoms of low self-esteem and a sense of worthlessness. In schizophrenia, the cognitive difficulties can involve hearing voices or experiencing visual delusions. The way a person feels and behaves will also differ, depending on the type of disorder. As emotion, cognition and behaviour all involve physiological changes within the body, it is reasonable to assume that there is a relationship between these processes.

Different approaches to treatments of mental disorder have focused on changing these four components of distress. A summary of these approaches and the aspect of mental distress they address is given in Figure 4.1. Each presents ethical and practical dilemmas for the mental health practitioner and the patient. This chapter describes and evaluates six treatment methods, and considers the rights and responsibilities of individuals and society in treating mental ill-health.

Approach	Focus
Learning theory	Changing the behaviour of the individual by providing role models
Behaviourism	Changing the behaviour of the individual through classical or operant conditioning
Cognitive	Changing the conscious thought processes of the individual
Psychodynamic	Revealing unconscious motivations to reduce emotional and physical distress
Humanistic	Creating the right environment to allow the individual to make changes in all aspects of life
Biological	Changing the physiology of the individual through medical treatments

Figure 4.1: A summary of the six treatment approaches

4.2 The social learning theory approach

Bandura (1969) claimed that individuals learn how to behave by observing same-sex role models of a slightly higher status to the observer. If the role model is rewarded (positively reinforced) for behaving in a particular way, then this increases the likelihood that the observer will imitate the behaviour. This process of social learning can be used to explain how individuals acquire mental health problems. For example, a young boy observes that his father is afraid of heights. Other people pay attention to his father when he shows this fear. The young boy imitates his father's behaviour, hence developing a phobia of heights.

Assumptions and influences on treatment method

There are five main assumptions of the social learning theory approach, as follows.

1. Mental distress is learned through interaction with the environment by a process of imitation, observation and reinforcement.

2. Behaviour has a direct impact on thoughts and feelings.

3. The thoughts and feelings of an individual will therefore change when behaviour changes.

4. The patient can be taught new ways of behaving, using role models to demonstrate appropriate behaviour.

5. There is no need to uncover the original cause of the disorder or take into account any physiological contributions.

Psychological difficulties may arise if the individual has imitated the behaviour of inappropriate role models.

Modelling

To change a patient's behaviour, the therapist acts as a role model, demonstrating more appropriate ways of responding. The process is known as modelling.

Study 4.1

AIM Bandura (1971) wanted to show that phobia can be treated using the modelling technique.

METHOD Patients with a phobia of snakes were shown demonstrations of a role model holding a snake. The therapist moved gradually closer to the snake while the patient observed. The role model remained fearless throughout. The patient was asked to imitate what the therapist was doing, performing the tasks at the same time. As participants became less fearful, the role model reduced his or her participation.

RESULT Bandura found that patients overcame their phobia and were eventually able to handle snakes without showing any fear response.

CONCLUSION Modelling is an effective method of treating phobias.

EVALUATIVE COMMENT

Modelling had been effective in treating anxiety and also helping to develop social skills (Bellack *et al.*, 1976). However, not all psychological problems can be treated by a role model demonstrating appropriate behaviour. For example, during the manic phase of bipolar disorder, the individual loses touch with reality. Modelling would therefore not be effective.

Modelling can
be an effective
way of treating
phobias

The original modelling approach did not consider cognitive processes. Meichenbaum (1971) found that learning was improved when the therapist talked about what they were doing in the therapy session. For example, during a problem-solving exercise the therapist might say 'Let's see, if I can't get anywhere, I'll try another way altogether.' Patients found it easier to understand what was needed when they heard the therapist think aloud, rather than simply observing the therapist's behaviour.

Bandura (1986) acknowledged the importance of cognitive processes and his later work contributed to the development of cognitive therapy.

4.3 The behaviourist approach

This approach centres on the belief that most forms of mental disorder occur as a result of maladaptive learning, through a process of either classical or operant conditioning.

Assumptions and influences on treatment methods

There are five main assumptions of the behaviourist approach, as follows.

1. Behaviour has a direct impact on thoughts and feelings.

2. The thoughts and feelings of an individual will change when behaviour changes.

3. There is therefore no need to examine the mind or thought processes of the patient.

4. The patient can be taught new ways of behaving using behavioural techniques.

5. When maladaptive learning is replaced by adaptive learning, the individual will recover.

The behaviourist approach believes that psychological disorders arise because the individual has learned self-defeating or ineffective ways of behaving. In treatment there is no need to understand the underlying cause of a disorder, or rely on forming a good relationship between therapist and client. Improvement can be objectively and reliably measured by observing behavioural change.

Flooding

This type of therapy uses classical conditioning. The patient is forced to confront the object or situation that causes distress. Continued exposure to the feared stimulus will eventually weaken and extinguish the fear response. For example, a person with a fear of heights would be taken to a cliff-top and physically prevented from running away. Eventually the fear response would fade away.

Study 4.2

AIM Wolpe (1973) described the use of flooding in helping someone overcome a phobia of cars.

METHOD A young woman was made to sit in the back of a car and driven around continuously for four hours.

RESULT Initially the patient was hysterical with fear. Eventually the fear response subsided. By the end of the journey it had completely gone.

CONCLUSION Flooding is an effective technique in the treatment of a phobia.

REFLECTIVE Activity

There are ethical problems in using a treatment like flooding. Outline how a behaviour therapist could use this technique and remain within the British Psychological Society's ethical guidelines. Can you think of any other problems with this method of treatment?

EVALUATIVE COMMENT

Emmelkamp *et al.* (1992) found that flooding is a successful technique in helping people overcome certain types of phobia. Other types of mental disorder, such as depression or schizophrenia, cannot be treated using flooding, because there is no obvious feared external stimulus to work with.

There are ethical difficulties with this treatment method because it can be a highly traumatic process. Some people might find the approach too difficult and this could result in their fear or anxiety being made worse.

Flooding works by confronting a feared stimulus; however, sometimes patients' anxiety is more abstract – for example, fear of failure. Wolpe (1958) appreciated the limitations of flooding and developed a new behavioural technique known as systematic desensitisation.

Systematic desensitisation

Jacobson (1929) realised that anxiety and relaxation appeared to be incompatible states. When individuals were put in a state of deep relaxation, they were not afraid of a frightening stimulus. As noted above, Wolpe (1958) applied this knowledge to devise a treatment technique called systematic desensitisation. The therapy works by dealing with patients' imaginary fears in a step-by-step manner.

Initially, the individual would be taught relaxation techniques, such as deep breathing. The therapist also educates the client about the body's stress response, explaining that the human body will automatically bring symptoms of anxiety under control, given time. When the client experiences anxiety, they are asked to wait for a few minutes to allow it to subside naturally.

Wolpe recognised that many of his patients had abstract fears rather than fears about real-life situations. He decided to ask his patients to imagine a series of anxiety-provoking situations. The patient would then work with the therapist to draw up a hierarchy of these events, producing a list of situations ranked from most difficult to cope with, down to least difficult. For example, a patient with social phobia, who is afraid of being embarrassed in a social situation, might find a public presentation very stressful. Talking to a friend on the telephone might be the least stressful activity.

The patient is then asked to imagine being in these situations, starting with the least stressful. If they experience any anxiety during this process, they are asked to use their newly developed relaxation techniques or simply to wait for the feeling to disappear. The approach works through classical conditioning. The client is learning to associate a new response with a previously distressing stimulus. Over a few sessions they can usually tolerate more and more difficult situations, working their way up the hierarchy. Wolpe found that the ability to cope with imaginary stressful situations also had an effect on the reduction of anxiety in real life. Patients are also asked to put themselves in challenging real-life situations as homework, in between therapy sessions. For the technique to be successful, the steps to recovery should be moderately challenging, yet achievable.

Further behavioural treatment methods have focused on the use of operant conditioning. This is where the therapist positively reinforces a desired change in the patient's behaviour. An example of this method, using a token economy with schizophrenic patients, is described on page 75. Alternatively, negative reinforcement can be used to persuade a patient to stop behaving in an undesirable way. An example of this is given in the treatment of eating disorders on page 50. A summary of the types of treatment available using the behaviourist approach is shown in Figure 4.3 below.

Name of treatment	Type of conditioning
Flooding or implosion	Classical – patient must face up to their fears in one session
Systematic desensitisation	Classical – patient must face up to their fears gradually over a series of sessions
Aversion therapy	Classical – an undesirable behaviour is associated with a negative outcome
Token economy	Operant – patient is reinforced for behaving in the desired way

Figure 4.3: A summary of treatments using the behavioural model

EVALUATIVE COMMENT

Research (Davison, 1968) has shown that systematic desensitisation is a very effective way of treating disorders where anxiety is the main symptom. However, the client must be motivated and prepared to experience some stress.

It is crucial that the therapist does a thorough assessment of the patient's anxieties to make sure that they are inappropriate. For example, a person who is afraid of public speaking might actually be a very poor public speaker! If this was the case, they would need help to develop skills, rather than treatment with systematic desensitisation.

The behavioural approach doesn't look for underlying causes and tends to focus on behaviour rather than thoughts and feelings. However, it has been successfully combined with cognitive approaches to create a treatment method called cognitive behaviour therapy (CBT).

4.4 The cognitive approach

The cognitive approach assumes that an individual creates psychological difficulties by thinking in negative and self-defeating ways.

Assumptions and influences on treatment

The cognitive approach to treatment of atypical behaviour includes the following assumptions.

- Everyone has the capability to think in a rational and logical way.
- People have a choice in how they perceive the world.
- Thought processes affect feeling and behaviour.
- If a person changes the way they think, feelings and behaviour will also change.
- The patient can be taught new ways of thinking, using cognitive therapy.
- When a person thinks more positively, they will recover.
- There is no need to focus on the past.

The therapy concentrates on the way the mind works, but aims to understand it in a scientific and methodical way. Individuals often need professional help to recognise and alter their own negative thought processes. The therapist has a directive role in this process, helping the individual to think differently.

Rational emotive therapy

Ellis (1958) developed a cognitive treatment known as rational emotive therapy. Ellis believed that emotional disorders were often caused by irrational thoughts (see Figure 4.4). The most common faulty beliefs experienced by people with mental health problems were as follows.

I am worthless unless I am competent at everything I try.
I must be approved of and loved by everyone I meet.
My unhappiness is always caused by external events; I cannot control my emotional response.
It is upsetting when things are not the way I would like them to be.
Certain people are thoroughly bad and should be severely blamed or punished for it.
Because something once affected my life, it will do so indefinitely.
There is always a perfect solution to human problems and it is awful if it is not found.
I should depend on others who are stronger than I am.
It is easier to avoid difficulties and responsibilities than face them.
If something unpleasant happens I should keep dwelling on it.

Figure 4.4: Some common irrational thoughts according to rational emotive therapists

Study 4.3

AIM Newark *et al.* (1973) wanted to discover if people with psychological problems had irrational attitudes.

METHOD Two groups of participants were asked if they agreed with the following statements, identified by Ellis as irrational.

(a) It is essential that one be loved or approved of by virtually everyone in the community.

(b) One must be perfectly competent, adequate and achieving to consider oneself worthwhile.

One group consisted of people who had been diagnosed with anxiety. The other group had no psychological problems. They were defined as 'normal'.

RESULT A total of 65 per cent of the anxious participants agreed with statement (a) compared to 2 per cent of non-anxious participants. For statement (b), 80 per cent of anxious participants agreed, compared to 25 per cent of non-anxious participants.

CONCLUSION People with emotional problems think in irrational ways.

Ellis put forward what he called the ABC model to explain how psychological disturbance developed. Individuals encounter activating events (A) or difficulties in life. This triggers beliefs (B) about those events. The beliefs can be rational and logical, or irrational and self-defeating. The belief system of an individual leads to certain consequences (C) that affect feelings and behaviour. The consequences of beliefs can be either positive or negative. An example of the ABC model can be seen in Figure 4.5.

(A) Activating event	
You receive a low mark for your psychology coursework	
(B) Beliefs (about A)	
Rational	**Irrational**
You could have put in more effort	You should always succeed
(C) Consequences (of B)	
Desirable emotion	**Undesirable emotion**
You feel a bit disappointed with yourself	You feel a total failure
Desirable behaviour	**Undesirable behaviour**
You work harder at your next assignment	You quit college

Figure 4.5: An example of the ABC model in action

Ellis believed that irrational beliefs make impossible demands on the individual, leading to anxiety, failure and psychological difficulty. He devised a cognitive therapy to challenge and change patients' attitudes and beliefs about themselves.

The patient (or client) is educated about the influence of thoughts on feelings and behaviour using the ABC model. The therapist must convince the client that emotional problems can be overcome by rationally examining negative thoughts.

When clients have recognised and analysed their self-defeating beliefs, they are taught how to substitute them with more realistic alternatives. The aim is to help individuals gain full acceptance, allowing for mistakes as well as successes in their life. The therapist will help the client understand that everyone has problems and that sometimes life can be quite difficult. People with psychological problems often overemphasise their own faults, believing that other people are much more competent. These unrealistic attitudes must be directly challenged.

Once the client has demonstrated a new attitude during a therapy session it must become part of their everyday thinking. Many cognitive therapists set homework for clients to provide more opportunities for positive, rational thinking. Ellis understood the importance of getting clients to behave differently, in order to test out new beliefs and learn to cope with disappointments. This is why the approach is sometimes referred to as cognitive behaviour therapy.

Ellis is quite a controversial figure. He believes the therapist is a 'nonsense annihilating scientist' who can quickly recognise any self-defeating, irrational attitudes. He is renowned for his very direct and confrontational style. He would argue with clients and use very blunt language to get his point across. For example, Ellis (1984) quotes the following response to a client: 'The same crap! It's always the same crap. Now, if you would look at that crap ... you would get better straight away!' He is not interested in 'long winded dialogues', which, he believes, are self-indulgent. Ellis argues there is no point in going over past history or even responding sympathetically. This only encourages the need for attention and sympathy, and reinforces negative thinking.

Client and counsellor in a one-to-one therapy session

Other rational emotive therapists do use a more supportive and subtle approach (Goldfried and Davison, 1976) although the focus remains on the client making changes to their irrational thoughts.

Aaron Beck (1976) devised a further cognitive therapy. His approach to depression is discussed in Chapter 3. While Ellis directly challenges irrational thoughts, Beck's technique asks patients to provide evidence that their negative thoughts are correct. If this proof is not forthcoming, the patient should be motivated to change the way they think. The approach is more collaborative and less direct. For example, if a patient believed he was a bad father, Beck would ask him to give examples and question whether he had ever acted like a good father. Ellis, on the other hand, might say 'So what? It's not the end of the world, not everyone is good at parenting.'

REFLECTIVE Activity

Using the ABC model, choose a recent activating event in your life (for example, failing your driving test). Think of an example of a rational and irrational belief in response to this event. What effect would this have on the emotional and behavioural consequences?

EVALUATIVE COMMENT

RET seems to be effective in treating anxiety disorders (Haaga and Davison, 1989). It has also produced behaviour change in patients who are self-demanding and feel guilty about not living up to these expectations (Brandsma et al., 1978).

However, there are ethical difficulties with the argumentative stance of the approach. For example, Rogers (1951) would argue that creating a supportive therapeutic relationship is a much more humane and productive way of treating patients.

RET assumes that all patients' thoughts are illogical and irrational. There are two difficulties with this idea. Fancher (1995) argued that irrational thoughts might actually be very logical to an individual, in terms of their own life experiences. Didion (1979) pointed out that many psychologically healthy people think in irrational and illogical ways. For example, lots of people plan how they will spend their lottery win (sometimes without even buying a ticket!).

4.5 The psychodynamic approach

Freud was the founder of the psychodynamic approach. He believed that the central cause for neurosis (or psychological difficulties) was repression (see *Advanced Psychology*, Pennington *et al.*, 2003). This involves forcing upsetting, threatening or unacceptable thoughts to the back of the unconscious mind. These thoughts are usually concerned with childhood memories and the conflicts between the instinctive desires of a young child and the wishes of their parents. The inability to express early trauma leads to a build-up of psychic energy, creating the symptoms of mental disorder.

Assumptions and influence on treatment

The psychodynamic approach includes the following assumptions.

- The personality is formed during the first five years of childhood.
- Early relationships, particularly with parents, are critical in personality formation.
- Traumatic experiences in childhood are associated with later mental health problems.
- These early experiences are stored in the unconscious mind, which the individual cannot access.

According to the psychodynamic perspective, the patient is unable to make sense of their own distress because the cause is hidden in their unconscious mind. The aim of the therapy is to uncover repressed conflict. Repressing inner conflicts takes up energy which could be used much more productively in the patient's life. Treatment releases the accumulated psychic energy, a process known as catharsis. The therapist uses Freudian theory to interpret what the patient says over a long period of one-to-one counselling sessions.

Treatment methods

FREE ASSOCIATION

The patient (or client) is asked to lie on a comfortable couch and say whatever comes into their mind, no matter how trivial or strange. The analyst (or therapist) sits behind the client, so that they are not distracted in any way. Freud believed that with enough practice, the client would be able uncover unconscious thoughts and feelings from the past. It might take a few sessions before the client was able to speak freely, because usually in conversation we carefully monitor what we say, screening out what seems unimportant. Once the client began to freely associate, the therapist would carefully analyse and interpret what was said. Sometimes, however, the therapist might observe some **resistance** to continue with free association.

RESISTANCE

Blocks to the process of psychoanalysis are known as resistance. Patients might suddenly dry up when they are speaking or appear unwilling to continue. Alternatively, they can quickly change the subject or start to tell jokes. Sometimes, patients 'forget' appointments or turn up late. Freud believed that any resistance to treatment was an indication that the analyst was getting closer to the source of the unconscious conflict.

TRANSFERENCE

Freud was also interested in the way the client acted towards the therapist. The patient's reactions and feelings towards the therapist (either negative or positive) could seem out of place. For example, they could become aggressive for no apparent reason, or very childlike. Freud believed that this response demonstrated a relationship from the client's past, rather than a reaction to the analyst. Attitudes from the past were being transferred onto the present. Transference was therefore another way of uncovering repressed memories. When analysts notice transference occurring they should respond in an emotionally neutral way. This will help the client to understand that the response is not caused by the therapist but actually reflects an earlier important relationship. They are transferring feelings about the past onto the present situation.

ANALYSIS OF DREAMS

The therapist would also ask the client to make a note of the content of their dreams. Freud thought that dreams were the 'royal road to the unconscious' and that repressed wishes often emerged in the form of dreams. He distinguished between what actually happened in the dream, known as the **manifest content**, and the underlying meaning, which is called the **latent content**. Even during dreams, Freud believed that the ego distorted or disguised unconscious instincts. Dreams therefore had to be carefully psychoanalysed, to reveal their true latent meaning.

INTERPRETATION

Free association, dream analysis and transference all depend on the therapist's interpretation of what the patient says. This must not be offered too soon in the process, as the client may not be ready to accept it. At the right time, the analyst begins to offer their interpretation. The patient can then start to examine repressed conflicts and unconscious desires, with the help and support of their therapist. It can be a very slow process, as the patient gradually accepts the analyst's interpretations and gains insight. This should eventually lead to a lasting personality change, allowing patients to deal with problems in a realistic and conscious way.

Study 4.4

AIM Freud (1909) presented a case history to exemplify the success of his psychoanalytic treatment. This is known as the case study of the 'Rat Man'.

METHOD A young soldier of 29 was given psychoanalysis for a period of 11 months. He had been told by a fellow officer about a terrible method of torture and began to worry obsessively that his father and his girlfriend might be punished in a similar way. To prevent his loved ones from coming to harm, he believed he had to perform a series of rituals. These were a set of self-imposed instructions, so complicated they were impossible to follow. Many of these rituals involved drawing up maps and timetables, and involved exploration. Freud believed that these neurotic searching symptoms were caused by an early childhood relationship. During analysis, the patient recalled that his governess had allowed him to explore her 'secret parts'. He also revealed that his father was already dead.

RESULT Freud concluded that this early sexual experience had created a feeling of guilt in the patient, making him feel he deserved to be severely punished. His early sexual development was therefore associated with extreme doubt. The punishment that he feared for others was actually an unconscious fear about being punished. Freud gave his interpretation to the patient, who subsequently recovered completely.

CONCLUSION Early childhood experiences can cause psychological difficulties in adulthood, and psychoanalytic treatment techniques can help uncover and deal with repression.

EVALUATIVE COMMENT

There are obvious problems with the sample size and ability to generalise from case studies. Critics have also questioned the reliability and accuracy of the information gathered because

Freud did not take careful notes during the therapy sessions (Davison and Neale, 2001). His recollections of what happened during therapy were made retrospectively and may have been biased by his own theoretical beliefs.

Freud was working at a time when knowledge and understanding about the brain was limited. Modern neuroscience has found no biological evidence of blocked psychic energy (Miller, 1999). However, some practitioners find the idea useful as a metaphor to explain how people experience psychological distress.

4.6 The humanistic approach

The humanist movement (see Pennington *et al.*, 2003) believes that psychological distress is created because of conflict between inner potential and the external demands of family, friends and society. Rogers called this state **incongruence**. Incongruence is a painful but positive state because it signals an awareness that the individual must change.

Assumptions and influences

The humanistic approach includes the following assumptions.

- Everyone is born with the potential to be successful and happy.

- Psychological problems result when external forces prevent an individual from reaching this potential.

- A supportive and encouraging therapist can help the patient to self-actualise. This is the process of recognising and reaching their own potential.

Humanists believe there is no need for interpretation during therapy. The client can work out the solution, given the right environment. The aim of the therapy is to create the therapeutic circumstances to help the patient make the right life choices.

Humanistic therapy

The central belief in humanistic therapy is that incongruence plays a major role in the development of mental health problems. Rogers believed the best way to reduce incongruence was to provide a supportive atmosphere. A good therapeutic environment is created by the following factors.

1. *Genuineness* – the therapist should be honest about their feelings during the session and not hide behind a professional mask. Rogers admitted he sometimes cried with clients when sad issues were being discussed. Most people can tell if someone is trying to hide their emotions, and tend not to believe them. By being genuine, the counsellor can develop mutual respect and trust.

2. *Unconditional positive regard* – clients should feel they can say or do what they want in the therapy sessions, without fear of being judged. The therapist must respect the goals and values of their clients. This unconditional positive regard promotes a sense of security, allowing the clients to recognise their own potential and make their own decisions about how to change their life for the better.

3. *Empathy* – the therapist should try to see the client's point of view and understand what they are feeling. To show empathy, the counsellor uses a technique called 'reflection', summarising what the client has said and feeding it back to them. For example, if the client says 'I felt anxious about seeing my boss this week', the therapist might reflect 'It sounds like you're worried about the opinions of others at work.'

Genuineness, unconditional positive regard and empathy are essential components to create a safe therapeutic environment for the client in humanistic therapy. Therapists use **active listening skills** to demonstrate these qualities during counselling. These skills include paying attention to the content of what is said, trying to understand the feelings involved, and reflecting this information back to the client. Rogers believed that active listening helped clients gain a greater understanding of their own feelings and should eventually enable them to decide how to change. The approach focuses on what is happening now and sees no value in looking back at the past to understand anxiety.

Although Rogers rejected the scientific approach, he did undertake empirical research to support his theories.

Study 4.5

AIM Rogers and Dymond (1954) wanted to provide evidence that the humanistic theory of personality and counselling were valid.

METHOD He used a Q sort technique with clients undergoing humanistic therapy. Each client was presented with a pile of cards with personal statements written on them. For example 'I am a friendly person' and 'I am often nervous'. The clients were asked to choose the cards that best described them (their real self) before counselling began. The procedure was repeated for the ideal self. Rogers calculated the gap between the statements. Clients were treated with humanistic therapy and the Q sort technique was used again.

RESULT Rogers found that self and ideal self had become more compatible after counselling.

CONCLUSION Humanistic therapy improves the self-concept and feelings of self-esteem of clients, which helps them to recover from psychological difficulty.

REFLECTIVE Activity

Could there be situations in counselling where it is difficult to show unconditional positive regard to a client? One example might be if the client makes racist comments. Can you think of other examples? How do you think a counsellor should respond if a client reveals something that has legal or moral implications?

EVALUATIVE COMMENT

As with all 'talking cures' clients must be able to articulate their feelings and be motivated to change. Biological treatments for anxiety do not require this level of committed effort and therefore may be more suitable for some patients.

The humanistic approach has been criticised for being over-optimistic about human nature. Rogers' claim that everyone is born basically good ignores the possibility of inherited individual differences in personality (Eysenck, 1994).

The claim that disturbance arises as a result of the negative influence of others has also been questioned. Freudian practitioners would argue that taking on the views of others is an essential part of healthy personality formation, ensuring that individual desires are kept in check.

4.7 Biological approach

The biological approach assumes that psychological difficulties are caused by physiology, such as brain chemistry, hormones, brain damage or genetic inheritance.

Assumptions and influences

The biological approach includes the following assumptions.

- Mental disorders can be understood as illness in the same way as physical conditions. They can be classified, diagnosed and treated by the medical profession in the same way as physical disease.

- The emphasis is on physiology rather than behavioural, cognitive or emotional difficulties.

- It is assumed that scientific research will eventually discover the biological causes of all types of mental disorder.

The approach is known as the medical model (see Chapter 1) and treatment involves bringing about physical changes in the patient using drugs, electro convulsive therapy (ECT) or brain surgery, rather than counselling or other forms of psychological treatment. These treatments are summarised in Figure 4.7.

Treatment	Possible side effects
Anxiolytic drugs	Addiction, withdrawal symptoms, possibility of overdose, rebound anxiety, drowsiness, tremors and convulsions
Antidepressant drugs	Reactions to certain foods, dry mouth, headaches, agitated state of mind, suicidal thoughts
Antipsychotic drugs	Blurred vision, grogginess, a shuffling gait, muscular rigidity
Electro convulsive therapy (ECT)	Headaches, nausea, loss of memory
Psychosurgery	Permanent changes to the personality, lethargy, death

Figure 4.7: Medical treatments and their side effects

Drug therapies

In the 1950s psychotropic drugs (which act on the brain and reduce the symptoms of mental disorders) were discovered. They were seen as a major breakthrough because they allowed patients to be treated by their own doctor and remain in their own homes.

ANTI-ANXIETY DRUGS (ANXIOLYTICS)

These minor tranquillisers help people to relax and reduce tension. They are very effective in reducing the symptoms of anxiety (see Chapter 2). Valium is a well-known anti-anxiety drug. However, anxiolytic drugs can be addictive, causing serious withdrawal problems if the patient tries to stop taking them. In the 1960s they were over-prescribed, particularly to women. Many patients took anti-anxiety drugs for a number of years, experiencing rebound anxiety whenever they tried to come off them. This is a type of anxiety that is even more intense than the original symptoms. The drugs can also have unpleasant side effects such as drowsiness, tremors and convulsions.

EVALUATIVE COMMENT

Anti-anxiety drugs are effective in reducing anxiety in the short term, and have also been used to help patients overcome withdrawal from drug or alcohol addiction. However, they are not really effective in treating those disorders where the anxiety occurs in spontaneous, sudden panic attacks.

Awareness of problems with dependency and withdrawal has changed the way anxiolytic drugs are used. Today they are prescribed for much shorter periods of time. When the patient starts to feel less anxious, the doctor carefully reduces the dose over a period of weeks, to reduce the likelihood of withdrawal symptoms.

ANTIDEPRESSANTS

These drugs help to elevate mood. As their name suggests, they are effective in treating depression (see Chapter 3). They have also been used to treat some anxiety disorders and bulimia nervosa, which is a type of eating disorder. Antidepressants work by acting on the chemistry of the brain.

The brain produces neurotransmitters to pass messages between different neurons in the brain and the nervous system. These brain chemicals transmit messages between neurons. The amount of certain neurotransmitters in the brain (noradrenaline and serotonin) may be reduced during depression (see Chapter 3). Antidepressants increase the levels of these neurotransmitters in the brain.

Early antidepressants had serious side effects such as an increased risk of a cerebral haemorrhage and dangerous reactions with certain foods, such as cheese. They also took three or four weeks to take effect. The most recent antidepressants to be developed are those that specifically target the neurotransmitter serotonin, known as selective serotonin reuptake inhibitors (SSRIs). Prozac is a well-known SSRI. These types of drugs have fewer side effects and are not fatal if the patient takes an overdose. SSRIs begin to have an effect after about two weeks.

EVALUATIVE COMMENT

Fisher and Greenberg (1995) found that antidepressants are effective when used in the short term with severe depression. However, over a period of time they seem to be less effective, suggesting that other more psychological methods, such as counselling, are also needed.

There has been some controversy surrounding the safety of Prozac recently. Healey (1999) claims that about 250 000 people worldwide have attempted suicide while taking Prozac, with 25 000 succeeding. Survivors have described a strange, agitated state of mind with unstoppable urges to commit violent acts. They had not felt suicidal prior to taking Prozac.

ANTIPSYCHOTIC DRUGS

These drugs are major tranquillisers, used to treat the most severe mental health problems, such as schizophrenia and manic depression (bipolar disorder). These disorders are characterised by dramatic (known as positive) symptoms, such as hearing voices or grandiose delusions, where the sufferer can mistakenly believe that they have an important role in the world. The patient becomes psychotic, losing touch with reality. Antipsychotic drugs tranquillise the patient without impairing consciousness, so that the bizarre thought processes gradually disappear. The treatment does not cure psychosis but reduces the symptoms over time. If a patient stops taking medication, the symptoms will return.

An early group of antipsychotic drugs, known as the **phenothiazines**, work by blocking the action of the neurotransmitter dopamine. They were developed in the 1950s and seen as a great breakthrough in treatment, allowing psychiatric patients (who were previously hospitalised for most of their lives) to live in the community.

EVALUATIVE COMMENT

Antipsychotic drugs are effective in treating the positive symptoms of schizophrenia but do not effect other symptoms such as depression, anxiety or guilt. (Klein and Davis, 1969).

Drug treatments do not cure the patient. To remain symptom free, the drugs must be taken continuously. Typically, patients are kept on a maintenance dose, which is just enough to continue the therapeutic effect. The dose is monitored and adjusted during visits to a psychiatric hospital. Many patients find the side effects of the drugs (see Figure 4.7) very difficult to accept and therefore stop taking their medication. This can result in what is known as the 'revolving door' pattern of admission. Patients are admitted to hospital, diagnosed and treated, discharged into the community and subsequently re-admitted. Hogarty et al. (1974)

found that combining drug treatment with social skills training, helped patients to fit into the community and prevented relapse.

Electro convulsive therapy (ECT)

Cerletti and Bini introduced a new method of treatment for severe mental health problems in

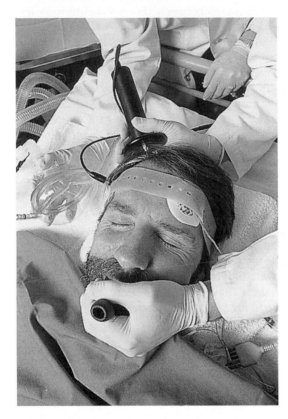

ECT is a controversial treatment for severe depression

1938. They gave an electric shock to the brain of a psychiatric patient, believing that it would eliminate symptoms of schizophrenia by producing an epileptic seizure. Early applications of this controversial treatment were administered without general anaesthetic and almost certainly used to subdue troublesome patients (Jarvis *et al.*, 2002).

ECT was later found to be more effective in treating severe depression than schizophrenia. Today, patients are given a fast-acting anaesthetic and a muscle relaxant, to prevent injury during the seizure. Electrodes are attached to the patient's temples and a 70 to 150 volt shock is given, lasting for up to one second. The shock produces a convulsion that lasts from 30 seconds to one minute. The patient regains consciousness about 15 minutes later.

ECT can be administered bilaterally, where electrodes are attached to both sides of the head, or unilaterally, where just one electrode is used. Unilateral ECT has fewer side effects but is less effective with severe depression (Benton, 1981). The treatment is usually given two or three times a week for up to four weeks. After treatment, the patient is confused, feels nauseous and has a headache. These side effects usually ease

within 40 minutes. There is often some retrograde amnesia, with the patient forgetting events prior to the ECT. Memory usually gradually returns in the following days.

Study 4.6

AIM Ng *et al.* (2000) wanted to investigate the effectiveness of ECT with patients suffering from severe depression.

METHOD Unilateral ECT was given to 32 patients over a six-week period of treatment.

RESULT Symptoms of depression decreased by around 50 per cent following treatment. Although memory was found to be seriously affected straight after treatment (over 30 per cent of personal memories were lost), patients recovered memories within the following month.

CONCLUSION Ng *et al.* concluded that ECT was an effective treatment for severe depression.

It is not known precisely how ECT works or why inducing a seizure reduces symptoms of severe depression. It may be that the treatment alters some of the brain's electrochemical processes (Benton, 1981). Alternatively, Milo *et al.* (2001) found that blood flow to the frontal lobes of the brain increased immediately after ECT, suggesting this might be how the treatment works.

EVALUATIVE COMMENT

Many critics of this treatment view it as unethical, especially as it can, in extreme circumstances, be administered against the person's will, if he or she is detained under the Mental Health Act.

Breggin (1991) presented two case histories to support his claim that ECT causes brain damage and is most often used with elderly women. He argued that the treatment causes anosognosia, a condition where the patient denies his or her own psychological difficulties.

Clare (1980) argued that because the treatment is relatively quick and easy to administer, that the psychiatric profession has over used it. Other researchers claim that it is not as successful as drug treatments (Youssef and Youssef, 1999), and believe it is time that psychiatry abandoned ECT all together.

PRACTICAL Activity

Summarise the six approaches to mental health care using Figure 4.9 as a template to help you.

Approach	Explanation of cause	Treatment methods
Biological	Disease, genetics, brain chemistry	Drugs, ECT or brain surgery
Psychoanalytic		
Behaviourist		
Learning theory		
Humanism		
Cognitive		

Figure 4.9: Summary of the approaches to mental health care

4.8 Evaluating the effectiveness of treatments

It is extremely difficult to compare the effectiveness of different therapies. This is because any differences between the groups could be due to individual differences in the severity of the disorder, age, gender, social class or the therapeutic relationship. In spite of these difficulties there has been some research to compare different treatment methods.

Study 4.7

AIM Elkin *et al.* (1985) investigated recovery rates in three different treatment groups for depression.

METHOD Researchers from six treatment centres recruited 240 out-patients suffering from depressive illness to take part in the research. Patients were randomly allocated to one of four treatment methods. One group received cognitive therapy, a second group was given psychodynamic therapy, a third group was treated with an antidepressant drug and the final group was given a **placebo**. This was a dummy drug, with no physiological affect on the depressive symptoms. They were told it might be effective as an antidepressant drug. All the patients were monitored for improvement over 16 weeks. A follow-up report was also undertaken 18 months after the treatment.

RESULT All three active treatment groups showed improvement when compared with the placebo group. Drug treatment produced the quickest recovery but after 16 weeks the other two treatment groups had caught up. The therapy groups were less likely to experience further episodes of depression than the patients who received medication.

CONCLUSION The inclusion of a placebo group clearly showed the advantage of receiving active treatment for depression. The study suggested that antidepressants are effective in the short term but that psychotherapy offers longer-term advantages.

EVALUATIVE COMMENT

The patients in Elkin's study were only moderately depressed. The findings cannot be generalised to more severe depression or other psychological disorders. Also, drop-out rates varied between the treatment methods and this may have biased the average level of recorded improvement.

The improvement rates in Elkin's study also varied across the six centres, suggesting that there were important differences in the way treatments were administered.

REFLECTIVE Activity

Do you think it is fair to use a placebo in treatments for mental health? What ethical considerations are there in this type of research?

4.9 Personal influences on choice of treatment

With such a wide range of treatment methods available, individuals have choices about what kind of psychological help they receive. However, many psychological or so called 'talking cures', such as psychoanalysis, are undertaken in private practice. A personal influence on the type of treatment chosen is economic. Private-practice psychotherapy can cost between £25 and £100 per 50-minute session. Treatment given without charge, by the National Health Service, adopts a more medical model, often involving the prescription of drugs.

Holmes (1994) argued that private patients tend to choose treatment methods that they feel comfortable with. For example, a very articulate client who was motivated to examine feelings might prefer a talking cure, such as client-centred therapy. A person with a more scientific approach to life might be more comfortable with a behavioural technique, where improvement can be objectively demonstrated.

Individuals often chose a therapist on the recommendations of others. Personal choice is therefore affected by interpersonal relationships with people in similar circumstances.

Mohr (1995) looked at a group of patients whose treatment had been unsuccessful. He found that patients who were poorly motivated, had poor interpersonal skills or thought therapy would be easy, were most likely to report negative outcomes.

EVALUATIVE COMMENT

Mohr's study found a correlation between patients' poor interpersonal skills and unsuccessful therapy; patients with poor skills were associated with negative outcomes. However, it is not necessarily a causal relationship. Also, the study was undertaken retrospectively (after treatment had failed). A further problem in locating reasons for treatment failure within the patient is that it ignores the role of the therapist.

Although patients appear to have choice in the treatments they receive, it is limited. Initially, most people experiencing difficulties consult their own doctor. He or she will usually prescribe drug treatments or refer the patient for further psychiatric assessment. Some doctor's surgeries

also provide a counselling service but this is unlikely to offer all of the different types of therapies available.

4.10 Cultural influences on choice of treatment

Culture is a socially transmitted set of ideas affecting an individual's way of seeing and thinking about the world. Lago and Thompson (1996) have written about the cultural values apparent in the wide range of theories about mental health.

Definitions of 'normal' behaviour

All of the approaches imply that there is a definition of normal behaviour that is more or less universal across social, cultural, economic and political backgrounds. Pedersen (1987) argued that white, male, middle-class mental health practitioners generally define normality. This may explain why women and black people receive more psychiatric diagnoses and medical treatments than other groups (see Chapter 1). The rights of different groups are protected by the Mental Health Act 1983. It states that individuals should receive respect for, and consideration of, their individual qualities and diverse backgrounds.

An emphasis on the individual

Many Westernised treatment methods for mental disorder focus on changing the individual and ignore the social context of distress. Individuals are perceived as capable of making the necessary changes within themselves, rather than receiving help to alter their external circumstances. Ussher (1989) cautioned against simply seeing psychological difficulty, such as depression, as an individual problem requiring analysis. She believed that depression is often a healthy reaction to an unjust situation.

Neglect of history

Medical and psychological treatments for mental health disorders are relatively recent. Pederson (1987) argued that many practitioners fail to acknowledge the ways in which people have solved problems over the previous thousand years. This leads to a tendency to try out the latest trend or fad with mental health patients.

Dependence on abstract words

Many psychological treatments have their own jargon that can be difficult for clients to understand. This is particularly true if an individual originates from another culture and English is not their first language. The Mental Health Act 1983 provides guidance for dealing with patients from a different cultural background. Whenever possible the patient should be assessed by someone from their own culture. If this is not practical, a trained interpreter should be made available.

Gilman (1985) highlighted that many mental health practitioners tend to perceive working-class patients as 'non-verbal' and therefore prescribe medical interventions rather than talking cures. Nash et al. (1965) challenged this cultural bias.

People often talk their problems over with friends

AIM Nash *et al.* (1965) wanted to measure the importance of shared expectations between therapists and clients.

METHOD Working-class patients were advised about what the treatment involved in a role induction interview at the start of therapy. The success of their treatment was compared to a control group of working-class clients who did not receive an induction.

RESULT The role induction group had a lower drop-out rate from the therapy than the control group. They also showed greater improvements than the control group as assessed by the patients and the therapists.

CONCLUSION Shared expectations about therapy can increase the effectiveness of the treatment.

Lago and Thompson (1996) have identified a series of questions to help develop cultural awareness in mental health practitioners. These are shown in Figure 4.11 below.

1. Do you understand the impact of your own history on assumptions about culture, identity and morals?
2. Do you understand the discriminatory nature and power imbalance between dominant and minority groups in society?
3. Can you enhance your own understanding about the culture of your clients?
4. Are you open to a range of challenging and contradictory views of the world as expressed by your clients?
5. How can theory and counselling be developed or changed to incorporate cultural differences?
6. Can you acknowledge the societal and political implications of the client's circumstances?

Figure 4.11: Lago and Thompson's cultural awareness training questions for therapists

EVALUATIVE COMMENT

The British Psychological Society codes and guidelines are periodically revised in the light of social and political change. This indicates that mental health care is subject to cultural values rather than being an objective, scientific discipline.

Awareness and respect for cultural difference is a challenge for all mental health workers, and a vital issue to consider in training and practice.

4.11 Societal influences on choice of treatment

A humane society must ensure that care and assistance is given to distressed and vulnerable individuals. Because of the very nature of mental disorders, this sometimes means going against the wishes of the individual. For example, a person suffering from delusions of grandeur may be quite happy with his own belief that he is the son of God and will steadfastly refuse treatment. By law, he can be detained and treated without consent.

The legal rights of mental health patients are governed by the Mental Health Act 1983. It deals with the compulsory reception, care and treatment of patients. In Section 1 of the Act, mental disorder is split into four categories: severe mental impairment, mental impairment, psychopathic disorder, and mental illness. An explanation of what these terms mean can be seen in Figure 4.12. The majority of assessments are made under the category of mental illness and yet the Act does not give a definition of this term.

The Act clearly states that people must not be seen as mentally disordered 'by reason only of promiscuity or other immoral conduct, sexual deviancy or dependence on alcohol or drugs'. In the past, women who had children outside marriage and homosexuals have been categorised as mentally ill. This statement is an important safeguard against further abuses of this nature. The use of alcohol and other substances might sometimes cause a mental health problem within the scope of the Act, but use of these substances alone does not.

Definition	Description
Severe mental impairment	A state of arrested or incomplete development of mind, which includes severe impairment of intelligence and social functioning, associated with abnormally aggressive or seriously irresponsible conduct
Mental impairment	A state of arrested or incomplete development of mind, which includes significant impairment of intelligence and social functioning, associated with abnormally aggressive or seriously irresponsible conduct
Psychopathic disorder	A persistent disorder or disability of mind, which results in abnormally aggressive or seriously irresponsible conduct
Mental illness	No definition given

Figure 4.12: The definitions of mental disorder given in the Mental Health Act 1983

Admission to hospital without consent

Section 2 of the Act provides the authority for someone to be detained in hospital for assessment for up to 28 days. This is intended to give sufficient time for a full examination of the person's mental health to be made. Treatment can also be given during this time. Section 2 is used when a person is being compulsorily admitted to hospital for the first time. If continued detention is needed after 28 days, then Section 3 is applied.

Section 3 provides the authority for someone to be detained in hospital without consent for treatment, for up to six months initially. At the end of that time the section may be renewed. It is usually imposed when an individual and their mental health problems are well known to medical staff. It involves a firm treatment plan, rather than the more open-ended assessment of Section 2.

The Act stipulates that compulsory assessment and treatment should only happen in the interest of the patient's own health or safety, or for the protection of other people. A Section 3 order can not normally be imposed if the patient's nearest relative objects to it.

Two doctors must decide whether the patient is suffering from a mental disorder and assess the seriousness of the condition. One of these doctors should usually know the patient, either as a GP or a hospital-based consultant. The doctors must also ensure that a hospital bed is available if the patient is admitted. An approved social worker (APW) must also be present to formally make an application for admission to hospital under Section 2 or 3. The APW has overall responsibility for coordinating the process and for getting the patient to hospital. If possible, the patient's nearest relative should also be contacted and informed of the application. Some of the issues the APW must consider are shown in Figure 4.13.

The patient's wishes and view of his or her own needs
His or her social and family circumstances
The risk of making assumptions based on a person's sex, social, cultural background or ethnic origin
The possibility of misunderstandings caused by other health conditions, such as deafness
The nature of the illness
What may be known about the patient by his or her nearest relative
The needs of the family or others with whom the patient lives
The need for others to be protected from the patient
The impact compulsory admission would have on the patient's life after discharge from detention

Figure 4.13: Issues to be considered by an approved social worker (ASW) when making an assessment of a patient under the Mental Health Act 1983

Occasionally, if there is a risk of the patient causing serious physical harm, the police may also attend.

Section 4 of the Act allows for emergency admissions and requires only one medical recommendation. However, the patient can only be detained for a maximum of 72 hours. During that time, the opinion of a second doctor must be given. If the second doctor also agrees, the Section 4 can be converted to a Section 2 order.

Treatments

The treatment methods allowed under a compulsory order are also governed by the Mental Health Act. Under Section 57, patients are protected against treatments that are potentially dangerous or life-threatening. For example, a doctor must have consent from the patient and a second opinion before undertaking any surgical operation to destroy brain tissue.

Section 58 sets out the treatments that can be given without consent. These are any medication for the person's mental health disorder and also electro convulsive therapy. In the case of ECT there must be a detailed plan of the number and frequency of treatments required. A second opinion must always be taken if the patient does not (or in some cases cannot) give consent. The appointed doctor must consult two people who have been professionally involved with the patient, one of whom must be a nurse. These professionals must agree with the treatment plan before it can be implemented.

EVALUATIVE COMMENT

The government is currently proposing new mental health laws because, under the current legislation, patients can only be forced to have treatment in hospital. With the advent of community care (see Chapter 3) and the closure of many large psychiatric hospitals, many mental health patients are self-medicating. There are no laws to ensure that they continue to take their medication while in the community. The Zito Trust – set up by Jayne Zito, whose husband was killed by a mental health patient – has welcomed plans to legislate for compulsory treatment orders in the community.

A second proposal involves the indefinite detention in psychiatric hospitals of people who have severe mental health disorders, without any prior history of danger to others.

REFLECTIVE Activity

How do you think legislation for compulsory treatments in the community could be enforced? What are the practical difficulties in managing the process?

Self-help groups and mental health organisations are campaigning against the proposals, believing that the new legislation will create further stigma and fear. They argue that the whole ethos of care in the community revolves around helping people with mental health problems to live ordinary lives and not to control them.

Study 4.9

AIM MIND is an organisation that helps individuals with mental health problems. It conducted a survey about the recently proposed changes to the Mental Health Act.

METHOD A total of 1001 participants were asked if they thought that the introduction of the new laws would deter them from seeking help if they felt depressed or were suffering from a mental health problem.

RESULT A total of 52 per cent of 15–24 year olds said they would not seek medical help under the new laws. 40 per cent of people in the lowest earnings groups would not go to a doctor for help. Both of these groups are more likely to experience mental health problems than other sections of the community.

CONCLUSION The proposed changes may deter people with mental health problems from seeking help and treatment.

4.12 Ethical dilemmas of practitioners in mental health care

There are a number of different practitioners in mental health care. For example, clinical psychologists, social workers, nurses, psychotherapists and psychiatrists can all be involved in the care and treatment of individuals with psychological difficulties. These practitioners are agents of change. They have a responsibility for planning and carrying out treatment programmes aiming to help individuals to change their thoughts, feelings and behaviour.

One ethical consideration involves who decides how to make these changes. Some practitioners working in the medical model, such as psychiatrists, may be involved in administering treatments to patients without their consent, under Section 2 or 3 of the Mental Health Act. Informed consent is also an issue in psychotherapy, according to Holmes (1994), because of the following issues:

1. Patients are in a very vulnerable psychological state at the onset of the therapy. This means they may be unable to make a balanced decision about the suitability of treatments.

2. The general public does not have a wide understanding or knowledge of the many different approaches to treatment available.

3. Some therapies, such as psychoanalysis, insist on a level of professional distance for certain techniques to work. This can make it difficult to strike a balance between the information needed to gain informed consent and what the therapist tells the patient before therapy begins.

A second ethical issue is whether a treatment aims to control an individual's behaviour, rather than helping the individual to change. For example, the use of a token economy system within an institution (a behaviourist approach, see page 75) involves reinforcing desired behaviour with a token that can be exchanged for privileges. The ethical difficulty arises in deciding who defines what is desirable behaviour. This is usually the staff operating the token economy system rather than the individual patients. Wachtel (1977) argued that these types of treatment are open to abuse, as the power to withdraw privileges from uncooperative patients lies with staff.

The notion of abuse in other treatments is a third ethical dilemma faced by practitioners in mental health care. Masson (1992) has been a very outspoken critic of psychotherapies. He claimed that the imbalance of power in the relationship between a client and therapist allows abuse and bullying to take place. When therapy is undertaken in private practice the therapist benefits financially from the relationship. Masson produced evidence of emotional, sexual and physical abuse of patients by their therapists.

EVALUATIVE COMMENT

There are no general training standards or a regulatory organisation to oversee the work of private practitioners in psychotherapy. This means there are no set standards to measure the effectiveness or success of particular treatment methods. Many practitioners agree that a framework of professional practice should be established.

PRACTICAL Activity

Imagine you have been given the task of drawing up standards for mental health practitioners. You could consider: the training and assessment of practitioners, how should their work be monitored or supervised, how do clients decide which type of therapy to have and how can effectiveness be measured. Are there any difficulties in having common guidelines for many different approaches?

4.13 Practical dilemmas of practitioners in mental health care

There are practical difficulties in evaluating the effectiveness of the varied treatment methods in mental health care.

1. *How is recovery defined?* Although the goal of any treatment is recovery, there are no agreed criteria for deciding when this has happened. Both clients and therapists have a vested interest in arguing that therapy has worked. Clients have devoted time and money to the process. This could bias their opinions. Therapists could be motivated to see improvement because it is what they are paid to do. Paul (1966) believed that recovery could be measured by looking at objective behaviour, physiological responses (such as heart rate) and self-report from the clients. Using a variety of methods to measure effectiveness should improve the reliability of the evaluation.

A second difficulty in measuring recovery is whether it is permanent or short-lived. Patients who appear to have improved after treatment may later experience a relapse. Long-term follow-up is needed, to ensure that the therapy has been effective. This in itself creates practical problems because it is time-consuming (and sometimes impossible) to keep track of previous patients. Also, relapse may be due to other events occurring in the patient's future life (such as bereavement) rather than a failure of the original therapy.

2. *Is recovery due to the treatment method or the characteristics of the therapist?* Sloane *et al.* (1975) found that the relationship with the therapist was implicated in successful outcomes (see Chapter 3). In particular, a sympathetic and encouraging counsellor was highlighted as a central factor in the recovery of patients undertaking behavioural and psychodynamic treatments.

3. *Is it possible to compare different approaches?* As we have already seen in this chapter, it is difficult to measure the success of any given form of treatment, and even more complicated to compare across different methods. Research that has attempted to do this has often produced contradictory results. For example, Elkin *et al.* (1985) found that intervention did contribute to recovery rates. Other research has been more dismissive of psychological treatments.

Study 4.10

AIM Eysenck (1952) investigated the effectiveness of talking cures such as psychoanalysis.

METHOD He reviewed recovery rates in five studies of psychoanalysis and 19 studies of eclectic (mixed) psychotherapy. He compared these with the recovery rates of patients who had received no therapy but were on a waiting list.

RESULT He claimed that approximately 44 per cent of patients treated with psychoanalysis recovered and 64 per cent of those treated with eclectic methods improved. This compared unfavourably with the 70 per cent who did not receive treatment, but nevertheless spontaneously recovered!

CONCLUSION Eysenck concluded that psychotherapy was ineffective. It achieved nothing that wouldn't have happened naturally, without intervention.

EVALUATIVE COMMENT

Eysenck excluded the patients who dropped out of psychoanalysis. He argued they were not cured, although he did not confirm this. If these patients stopped coming because they were better, the success rate of psychoanalysis would have risen to 66 per cent.

Bergin and Lambert (1978) found that certain types of disorder, such as depression or anxiety, were more likely to disappear with time. Other conditions, such as obsessive compulsive disorder, were more likely to need some form of treatment. Further research is needed to investigate whether different treatments are more successful with certain disorders than others.

PRACTICAL Activity

Summarise the dilemmas surrounding the treatment and care of mental health patients from (a) the patient's perspective, (b) the professional's perspective, and (c) the legal perspective.

4.14 Sample questions

SAMPLE QUESTION

(a)   Identify and discuss one limitation of the behaviourist approach to treatment of atypical behaviour.
(AO1 = 2, AO2 = 2)   *(4 marks)*

(b)   Anne is an only child whose parents do not socialise a lot. She feels uncomfortable in crowded places, particularly around other children, and becomes very anxious at school, tending to avoid contact with children altogether.

Name and describe one technique a behaviour therapist might use to treat Anne.
(AO1 = 4)   *(4 marks)*

(c)   'A person who is severely mentally ill may be a danger to himself or herself and must be put into a psychiatric hospital.'

'A person who suffers from mental illness has the right to decide what treatment he or she has.'

With reference to the above statements, discuss the rights and responsibilities of individuals and/or society to determine treatments of atypical behaviour.
(AO1 = 4, AO2 = 8)   *(12 marks)*

Total AO1 marks = 10 Total AO2 marks = 10 Total = 20 marks

QUESTIONS, ANSWERS AND COMMENTS

(a)   Outline one assumption of a humanist approach to treatment of atypical behaviour.
(AO1 = 4)   *(4 marks)*

(b)   Outline one technique used in humanistic therapy and explain how this technique is influenced by one of the assumptions you have identified in your answer to part (a).
(AO1 = 2, AO2 = 2)   *(4 marks)*

(c)   Discuss at least two problems involved in assessing the effectiveness of therapies for the treatment of atypical behaviour. Refer to empirical evidence in your answer.
(AO1 = 4, AO2 = 8)   *(12 marks)*

Total AO1 marks = 10 Total AO2 marks = 10 Total = 20 marks

Answer to (a)

The humanist approach assumes that everyone is born with potential, but that taking on the views of others can prevent this potential being reached. In treatment, the therapist must try to create the right environment for the patient to make their own decisions rather than always trying to please other people. The therapy is very non-directive because the therapist does not tell the patient what to do.

Comment: This is a good answer, which gives an outline and expansion of the assumptions; full marks (4) awarded.

Answer to (b)

The therapist will use unconditional positive regard during therapy to help create the right environment for the client to change. This means he or she will not be judgemental or criticise the client in anyway.

Comment: This is a rather short answer, which does link to the assumption made in part (a). To achieve full marks the answer should consider the techniques used in therapy to show unconditional positive regard, such as empathy and genuineness. 1 mark awarded for AO1 and 1 for AO2.

Answer to (c)

There are problems in trying to assess the effectiveness of treatments because it is difficult to define what recovery means. There are no agreed criteria to measure recovery, and clients who seem to be better after treatment might relapse later. However, this might be because of subsequent events in the patient's life (like losing a job) rather than a failure of the treatment method. Longitudinal studies to follow-up patients would also be very time consuming. Paul thought that measurement of effectiveness could be made using a variety of methods, like physical responses, behaviour change and self-reports from clients.

Any differences in recovery rates might be due to the therapist rather than the type of treatment. For example, a supportive therapist has been shown to be an important factor in successful outcomes.

It is also difficult to compare different approaches. Eysenck found that talking cures such as psychoanalysis were no more effective than leaving the clients to recover on their own; 70 per cent of patients on a waiting list for therapy spontaneously recovered compared to a recovery rate of 44 per cent for psychoanalysis. However, Eysenck's research has been criticised because he excluded patients who dropped out. Some disorders might be easier to treat than others or would disappear with time. Further research could investigate whether different treatments are more effective with different disorders.

Comment: Three problems are discussed in this answer, although the description is very brief in one of them. Some empirical evidence and critical analysis is given with Eysenck's study. The use of a further study would improve the marks given: 8 marks awarded (3 for AO1 and 5 for AO2).

Sample questions, answers and comments

4.15 FURTHER READING

Introductory texts

Davison, G.C. & Neale, J.M. 2001: **Abnormal Psychology**. 8th Ed. Wiley, New York

Pennington, D.C., McLoughlin, J., Robinson, D. & Smithson, R. 2003: **Advanced Psychology. Child Development, Perspectives, Debates and Research Methods**. Hodder & Stoughton, London

Specialist sources

Department of Health and Welsh Office 1983: Code of Practice, Mental Health Act, HMSO, London

Gross, R. & McIlveen, R. 1999: **Therapeutic Approaches to Abnormal Behaviour**. Hodder & Stoughton, London

Jarvis, M., Putwain, D., & Dwyer, D. 2002: **Angles on Atypical Psychology**. Nelson Thornes, Cheltenham

Useful websites

www.mind.org.uk Information on mental health

www.news.bbc.co.uk Go to health/medical notes for up-to-date articles on all aspects of mental health

www.sane.org.uk Information on mental health

Glossary

Active listening skills A method of responding to a client in humanistic therapy, which indicates acceptance of the client's thoughts and feelings.

Androgynous Showing the characteristics of males and females, indistinguishable as either sex.

Anosognosia A perceptual disorder where an individual denies his or her psychological difficulties.

Anti-psychiatry movement A group of critics of the medical model of mental illness.

Antipsychotic drugs Psychoactive drugs that reduce psychotic symptoms but can have long-term side effects.

Asylum A large building created to house the mentally ill.

Atypical psychology Behaviour that is out of the ordinary, often indicating mental health problems.

Autonomy Independence of thought and action.

Avolition A negative symptom in schizophrenia where the individual lacks interest and drive.

Bedlam A term used to describe chaos or uproar.

Classical conditioning A basic form of learning in which a neutral stimulus is repeatedly paired with another stimulus known as the unconditioned response. The neutral stimulus becomes associated with the conditioned stimulus and elicits the same response.

Cognitive behaviour therapy (CBT) Behaviour therapy incorporating theory and research on cognitive processes such as negative thoughts, judgements and perceptions.

Cognitive restructuring A method of changing an individual's thought processes.

Community care A method of treating individuals with mental health problems in their own homes.

Concordance The similarity in psychiatric diagnosis, or in other traits, within a pair of twins.

Cultural bias A tendency to favour your own cultural view of the world.

Culture The set of beliefs, values and attitudes shared by most members of a community.

Delusion Beliefs that are contrary to reality.

Dementia praecox An early term used to describe the symptoms of schizophrenia.

Demonology Belief that an evil spirit has taken over the mind and body of an individual.

Developmental norm The type of behaviour that is expected at a given age.

Diathesis stress model The view that an individual is biologically predisposed towards a particular mental disorder and is particularly affected by stress. The disorder emerges if stress occurs.

Dopamine A neurotransmitter identified as a possible causal factor in the emergence of schizophrenia.

Double bind An interpersonal situation in which an individual is confronted, over a long period of time, by contradictory messages and requests from family members.

Electro convulsive therapy (ECT) A treatment method for severe depression, which involves passing an electrical current through the brain.

Enmeshed family A way of interacting within a family where individual members are over involved and lacking in autonomy.

Flat affect A lack of emotional response, whatever the stimulus.

Free association A procedure used in psychoanalysis to encourage the client to access repressed information.

Functional disorder An illness affecting the way an individual functions, with no clear physical cause.

General paresis A common mental disorder in the early twentieth century, found to be caused by venereal disease.

Hallucination A disturbance in perception, which can be auditory, tactile or visual.

Hierarchy A way of grading situations in behavioural treatments, with the least frightening situation at the bottom and the most frightening at the top.

Hyperventilation Breathlessness.

Idiographic Considering the unique characteristics of an individual.

Incongruence An imbalance between an individual's own needs and wishes and the needs and wishes of others.

Interactionist Combining both psychological and physiological knowledge and understanding to explain the causes of mental health problems.

Latent content The interpretation of the actual contents of a dream using Freudian theory. The presumed true meaning of a dream.

Learned helplessness A theory that individuals learn to be passive because they have experienced failure or unpleasant circumstances that they could not effectively control.

Leucotomy A surgical procedure that involves cutting away the brain tissue connecting the frontal lobes.

Maladaptiveness A term used to describe behaviour, thoughts or feelings that interfere with an individual's progress in the world.

Manic depression A term used to describe the mood swings seen in bipolar disorder.

Manifest content The actual contents of a dream.

Monoamine oxidase An enzyme that deactivates neurotransmitter activity after neural firing.

Moral treatment A humane way of treating people with mental health problems, involving peace and quiet.

Multi-axial classification system A method of rating an individual's mental health using five separate scales.

Multi-disciplinary Professionals from different disciplines, such as social work or nursing, working together.

Negative reinforcement Outlining the negative consequences if behaviour does not change in a desired direction.

Negative schemas Mental representations of the self, the world and the future, which are pessimistic.

Negative symptoms Behavioural deficits in schizophrenia, such as flat affect or avolition.

Neurosis A term used to describe a mental health problem where the individual is aware that their behaviour is unusual or distressed.

Neurotic anxiety Anxiety caused by psychological conflict.

Neurotransmitter A chemical substance used to transfer a nerve impulse from one neuron to another.

Nomothetic Relating to universal principles that can be applied to everyone.

Noradrenaline A neurotransmitter implicated in the onset of depression.

Objective anxiety Anxiety with an obvious, realistic, external cause.

Operant conditioning Changing behaviour because of a reward or to avoid a punishment.

Operational diagnostic criteria Information about the type and the number of symptoms that should be apparent before a diagnosis can be made.

Organic disorders Illnesses with a clear physical cause.

Palpitations A racing heartbeat.

Panic attacks Distressing episodes of extreme anxiety.

Phenothiazines A group of antipsychotic drugs that block dopamine receptors in the brain.

Phototherapy A treatment using powerful light therapy for seasonally affective disorder (SAD).

Placebo A dummy treatment method where the individual expects to experience a change in behaviour, thoughts or feelings.

Positive reinforcement Reward for a desired change in behaviour.

Positive symptoms In schizophrenia, behavioural excesses such as hallucinations and bizarre behaviour, not seen in everyday life.

Psychiatrist A medically trained doctor who has specialised in the area of mental health.

Psychogenesis The belief that mental health problems are caused by psychological rather than physical factors.

Psychosis A term used to describe a severe mental health problem where the individual loses contact with reality.

Psychotherapy A social interaction where a trained professional tries to help another person feel or think differently.

Psychotropic drugs A term used to describe drugs that have an effect on mood or thought processes.

Resistance A term used in psychoanalysis to describe blocks in progress.

Reuptake A process by which neurotransmitters are pumped back in to the producing neuron after neural firing.

Rituals Repetitive behaviour, often used to reduce the symptoms of anxiety.

Secondary symptoms Symptoms arising as a consequence of receiving a diagnosis of schizophrenia, such as depression or failing interpersonal relationships.

Self-actualisation Fulfilling one's potential.

Self-fulfilling prophecy A change in an individual's behaviour because of the expectations and responses of those around them.

Serotonin A neurotransmitter implicated in the onset of depression.

Situational norm The type of behaviour expected in a given situation.

Somatogenesis The belief in physical causes of mental ill-health.

Stereotype A widely held assumption about the personality, characteristics or behaviour of an individual based on group membership.

Subculture A section of society that holds different views and attitudes to the dominant culture.

Syndrome Symptoms that regularly appear together in a disorder.

Systematic desensitisation A behavioural treatment where the individual is required to face feared stimuli in a step-by-step manner.

Bibliography

Bandura, A. (1969) *Principles of Behaviour Modification*, New York, Holt, Rinehart & Winston

Bandura, A. (1971) *Social Learning Theory*, Morristown NJ, General Learning Press

Bandura, A. (1986) *Social Foundations of Thought and Action: A Social Cognitive Theory*, Englewood Cliffs NJ, Prentice Hall

Barlow, D.H. (1986) Causes of sexual dysfunction: the role of anxiety and cognitive interference, *Journal of Consulting and Clinical Psychology* 54, 140-8

Barlow, D.H. and Durand, V.M. (1995) *Abnormal Psychology: An Integrative Approach*, New York, Brooks Cole

Bateson, G., Jackson, D.D., Haley, J. *et al.* (1956) Toward a theory of schizophrenia, *Behavioural Science* 1, 251–64

Beck, A.T. (1976) *Cognitive Therapy and the Emotional Disorders*, New York, International Universities Press

Beck, A.T. (1987) Cognitive models of depression, *Journal of Cognitive Psychotherapy: An International Quarterly* 1, 5–37

Beck, A.T., Rush, A.J., Shaw, B.F. and Emery, G. (1979) *Cognitive Therapy of Depression*, New York, Guildford Press

Beck, A.T., Emery, G. and Greensberg, R.L. (1985) *Anxiety Disorders and Phobias: A Cognitive Perspective*, New York, Basic Books

Beitman, B., Goldfried, M. and Norcross, J. (1989) The movement toward integrating psychotherapies: an overview, *American Journal of Psychiatry* 146, 138–47

Bellack, A.S., Hersen, M. and Turner, S.M. (1976) Generalisation effects of social skills training in chronic schizophrenics: an experimental analysis, *Behaviour Research and Therapy* 14, 391–8

Bemis, K.M. (1978) Current approaches to the aetiology and treatment of anorexia nervosa, *Psychological Bulletin* 85, 593–617

Bentall, R.P, Haddock, G. and Slade, P.D. (1994) Cognitive behaviour therapy for persistent auditory hallucinations from theory to therapy, *Behaviour Therapy* 25, 51–66

Benton, D. (1981) Can the system take the shock? *Community Care* 12, March, 15–17

Bergin, A.E. and Lambert, M.J. (1978) The evaluation of therapeutic outcomes. In A.E. Bergin and S.L. Garfield (eds) *Handbook of Psychotherapy and Behaviour Change*, New York, Wiley

Bini, L. (1938) Experimental researches on epileptic attacks induced by electric current, *American Journal of Psychiatry Supplement* 94, 172–83

Brandsma, J.M., Maultsby, M.C. and Welsh, R. (1978) Self-help techniques in the treatment of alcoholism, in G.T. Wilson and K.D. O'Leary, *Principles of Behaviour Therapy*, Englewood Cliffs NJ, Prentice Hall

Breggin, P. (1991) *Toxic Psychiatry*, London, HarperCollins

Breslau, N., Holmes, J.P., Carlson, D.C. and Pelton G.H. (1998) Trauma and post traumatic stress disorder in the community, *Archives of General Psychiatry* 55, 626–32

Brewerton, T.D., Lydiard, B.R., Laria, M.T., Shook, J.E. and Ballenger J.C. (1992) CSF beta endorphin in bulimia nervosa, *American Journal of Psychiatry* 149, 1086–90

Bromley, J. (2002) Psychiatry Today, Royal College of Psychiatrists Annual Conference

Broverman, I., Broverman, D., Clarkson, F., Rosenkrantz, P. and Vogel, S. (1970) Sex role stereotypes and clinical judgements of mental health, *Journal of Consulting Psychology* 34, 1–7

Brown, G.W. and Harris, T.O. (1978) *Social Origins of Depression: A Study of Psychiatric Disorder in Women*, London, Tavistock

Brown, G.W, Bone, M., Dalison, B. and Wing, J.K. (1966) *Schizophrenia and Social Care*, London, Oxford University Press

Clare, A. (1980) *Psychiatry in Dissent*, London, Tavistock

Clark, D.F. (1988) The validity of measures of

cognition: a review of literature, *Cognitive Therapy and Research* 12, 1–20

Clark, D.M. (1986) Cognitive therapy of anxiety, *Behavioural Psychotherapy* 14, 283–94

Cochrane, R. (1987) *Social Creation of Mental Illness*, Harlow, Longman

Cochrane, R. (1995) Women and depression, *Psychology Review* 2, 20–4

Cochrane, R. and Stopes Roe, M. (1980) Factors affecting the psychological symptoms in urban areas of England, *Acta Scandinavia* 61, 445–60

Cooper, J.E. (1994) Notes on unsolved problems. In *Pocket Guide to ICD 10 Classification of Mental and Behavioural Disorders*, London, Churchill Livingstone

Davis, J.M. (1974) A two-factor theory of schizophrenia, *Journal of Psychiatric Research* 11, 25–30

Davison, G.C. (1968) Systematic desensitisation as a counterconditioning process, *Journal of Abnormal Psychology* 73, 91–9

Davison, G.C. and Neale, J.M. (1990) *Abnormal Psychology*, 5th edition, New York, Wiley

Davison, G.C. and Neale, J.M. (2001) *Abnormal Psychology*, 8th edition, New York, Wiley

Deep, A.I., Lilenfield, L.R., Plotnicov, K.H., Police, C. and Kaye, W.H. (1999) Sexual abuse in eating disorder subtypes and control women, *International Journal of Eating Disorders*

De Jong, W. and Kleck, R.E. (1986) *The Social Psychological Effects of Overweight. Physical Appearance, Stigma and Social Behaviour*, Hillside NJ, Erlbaum

Deutsch, A. (1949) *The Mentally Ill in America*, New York, Columbia University Press

Didion, J. (1979) *The White Album*, New York, Simon & Schuster

Eating Disorders Association (2000) *The Need for Action in 2000 and Beyond*, London, EDA

Elkin I. (1989) General effectiveness of treatments, *Archives of General Psychiatry* 46, 971–83

Elkin, I., Shea, T., Imber, S., Pilkonis, P., Sotsky, S., Glass, D., Watkins, J., Leber, W. and Collins, J. (1985)

NIMH treatment of depression collaborative research programme: initial outcome findings. Paper presented at meetings of the American Association for the Advancement of Science, May

Ellis, A. (1958) *Rational Psychotherapy*, Seacus NJ, Kyle Stuart

Ellis, A. (1984) Rational-emotive therapy. In R. Corsini (ed.) *Current Psychotherapies*, 3rd edition, Itasca, Peacock

Emmelkamp, P.M.G., Bouman, T.K. and Scholing, A. (1992) *Anxiety Disorders: A Practitioners Guide*, New York, Plenum

Eysenck, H.J. (1952) The effects of psychotherapy: an evaluation, *Journal of Consulting Psychology* 16, 319–24

Eysenck, M. (1994) *Individual Differences Normal and Abnormal*, Hove, Lawrence Erlbaum Associates

Fairburn, C.G. (1985) Cognitive behavioural treatment for bulimia. In D.M. Garner and P.E. Garfinkel (eds) *Handbook of Psychotherapy for Anorexia Nervosa and Bulimia*, New York, Guilford Press

Fancher, R.T. (1995) *Cultures of Healing*, New York, WH Freeman

Faulkner, A. and Layzell, S. (2000) Strategies for Living: The Research Report. A report of user-led research into people's strategies for living with mental distress, London, Mental Health Foundation

Fisher, S. and Greenberg, R. (1995) *A Critical Appraisal of Biological Treatments for Psychological Distress: Comparisons with Psychotherapy and Placebo*, Hillsdale NJ, Erlbaum

Freud, S. (1909) *The Complete Works of Sigmund Freud*, London, Hogarth Press

Freud, S. (1917) Mourning and melancholia, republished in J. Strachey (ed.) *The Standard Edition of the Complete Works of Sigmund Freud*, London, Hogarth Press

Freud, S. (1936) *The Problem of Anxiety*, New York, Norton

Frith, C.D. (1992) *The Neuropsychology of Schizophrenia*, Hove, Lawrence Erlbaum

Furnham, A. and Baguma, P. (1994) Cross-cultural differences in the evaluation of male and female body shapes, *International Journal of Eating Disorders* 15, 81–9

Garfield, S. (1980) *Psychotherapy: An Eclectic Approach*, New York, Wiley

Garner, D.M. and Bemis, K.M. (1982) A cognitive behavioural approach to anorexia nervosa, *Cognitive Therapy and Research* 6, 123–50

Garner, D.M, Garfinkel, P.E, Schwartz, D. and Thompson, M. (1980) Cultural expectations of thinness in women, *Psychological Reports* 47, 483–91

Gilman, S.A. (1985) *Difference and Psychopathology: Stereotypes of Sexuality, Race and Madness*, Ithaca, Cornell University Press

Goldfried, M.R. and Davison, G.C. (1976) *Clinical Behaviour Therapy*, New York, Holt, Rinehart & Winston

Gottesman, I.I. and Shields, J. (1972) *Schizophrenia and Genetics: A Twin Study Vantage Point*, New York, Academic Press

Green, B.L. (1994) Psychosocial research into traumatic stress: an update, *Journal of Traumatic Stress* 7, 341–63

Gross, R. (2001) *Psychology: The Science of Mind and Behaviour*, 4th edition, London, Hodder & Stoughton

Gross, R. and McIlveen, R. (2000) *Psychopathology*, London, Hodder & Stoughton

Haaga, D.A. and Davison, G.C. (1989) *Outcome Studies of Rational Emotive Therapy*, New York, Academic Press

Harrison, P. (1995) Schizophrenia: a misunderstood disease, *Psychology Review* 2, 2–6

Hawton, K., Salkovis, P.M., Kirk, J. and Clark, D.M. (1989) *Cognitive Behaviour Therapy for Psychiatric Problems*, Oxford, Oxford Medical Publications

Healey, D. (1999) *Psychiatric Drugs Explained*, Kings Lynn, Mosby

Herbert, J.D. (1995) An overview of the current status of social phobia, *Applied Preventive Psychology* 4, 39–51

Heston, L.L. (1966) Psychiatric disorders in foster-home-reared children of schizophrenic mothers, *British Journal of Psychiatry* 122, 819–25

Ho, B.C, Nopoulos, P., Flaum, M., Arndt, S. and Andreasen, N.C. (1998) Two year outcome in first episode schizophrenia: predictive value of symptoms for quality of life, *American Journal of Psychiatry* 155, 1196–201

Hogarty, G.E., Goldberg, S.C., Schooler, N.R., Ulrich, R.F. and the Collaborative Study Group (1974) Drug and sociotherapy in the aftercare of schizophrenic patients. Two year relapse rates, *Archives of General Psychiatry* 31, 603–8

Hogg, M.A. and Vaughan, G.M. (1995) *Social Psychology: An Introduction*, Hemel Hempstead, Prentice Hall

Holland, A.J., Hall, A., Murray, R., Russell, G.F.M. and Crisp, A.H. (1984) Anorexia nervosa. A study of 34 twin pairs and one set of triplets, *British Journal of Psychiatry* 145, 414–19

Holmes, D.S. (1994) *Abnormal Psychology*, 2nd edition, New York, HarperCollins

Hsu, L.K. (1990) *Eating Disorders*, New York, Guildford Press

Hugdahl, K., Fredrikson, M. and Ohman, A. (1977) Preparedness and arousability as determinants of electrodermal conditioning, *Behaviour Research and Therapy* 15, 345–53

Humphrey, L.L. (1989) Observed family interactions among subtypes of eating disorders using structured analysis of social behaviour, *Journal of Counselling and Clinical Psychology* 57, 206–14

Iversen, L.L. (1979) The chemistry of the brain, *Scientific American* 241, 134–49

Jacobson, E. (1929) *Progressive Relaxation*, Chicago, University of Chicago Press

Jarvis, M, Putwain, D. and Dwyer, D. (2002) *Angles on Atypical Psychology*, Cheltenham, Nelson Thornes

Jones, M.C. (1924) A laboratory study of fear. The case of Peter, *Pedagogical Seminary* 31, 308–15

Kaiser, A.S., Katz, R. and Shaw, B.F. (1998) Cultural issues in the management of depression. *Culture, Clinical Psychology and Theory Research and Practise*, New York, Oxford University Press

Katz, H.M. and Gunderson, J.G. (1990) Individual psychodynamically oriented psychotherapy for schizophrenic patients. In M.I. Hertz, S.J. Keith and

J.P. Docherty J (eds) *Handbook of Schizophrenia: Psychosocial Treatment of Schizophrenia*, Amsterdam, Elsevier Science Publishers, 69–90

Kety, S.S. (1974) From rationalisation to reason, *American Journal of Psychiatry* 131, 957–63

Kimble, D.P. (1988) *Biological Psychology*, New York, Holt, Rinehart & Winston

King, D.W., King, L.A., Foy, D.W., Keane, T.M. and Fairbank, J.A. (1999) Post traumatic stress disorder in a national sample of female and male Vietnam veterans: risk factors, war zone stressors and resilience-recovery variables, *Journal of Abnormal Psychology* 198, 164–70

Klebanoff, L.D. (1959) A comparison of parental attitudes of mothers of schizophrenics, brain injured and normal children, *American Journal of Psychiatry* 24, 445–54

Klein, D.F. and Davis, J.M. (1969) *Diagnosis and Drug Treatment of Psychiatric Disorders*, Baltimore, Williams Wilkins

Klerman, G.L. and Weissman, M.M. (1993) *New Applications of Interpersonal Psychotherapy*, New York, Basic Books

Klerman, G.I., Weissman, M.M., Rounsaville, B.J. and Chevron, E.S. (1984) *Interpersonal Psychotherapy of Depression*, New York, Basic Books

Korchin, S.J. (1976) *Modern Clinical Psychology*, New York, Basic Books

Kraeplin, E. (1981 [1896]) *Clinical Psychiatry* (trans. A.R. Diefendorf), Delmar NY, Scholars Facsimiles and Reprints

Lago, C. and Thompson, J. (1996) *Race, Culture and Counselling*, Milton Keynes, Open University Press

Laing, R.D. (1967) *The Politics of Experience and the Bird of Paradise*, Harmondsworth, Penguin

Levine, E.S. and Padilla, A.M. (1980) *Crossing Cultures in Therapy: Counselling for the Hispanic*, Monterey CA, Brooks Cole

Lewinsohn, P.M. (1974) A behavioural approach to depression. In R. Friedman and M. Katz (eds) *The Psychology of Depression: Contemporary Theory and Research*, Washington DC, Winston Wiley

Lewis, G., Croft-Jeffreys, C. and David, A. (1990) Are British psychiatrists racist? *British Journal of Psychiatry* 157, 410–15

Lin, E. and Kleinman, A. (1988) Psychopathology and the clinical course of schizophrenia: a cross cultural perspective, *Schizophrenia Bulletin* 14, 555–67

Littlewood, R. (1980) Anthropology and psychiatry: an alternative approach, *British Journal of Medical Psychology* 53, 213–25

Littlewood, R. and Cross, S. (1980) Ethnic minorities and psychiatric services, *Sociology of Health and Illness* 2, 194–201

Littlewood, R. and Lipsedge, M. (1989) *Aliens and Alienists. Ethnic Minorities and Psychiatry*, 2nd edition, London, Unwin Hyman

Lopez, S.R. and Hernandez, P. (1986) How culture is considered in evaluations of psychopathology, *Journal of Nervous and Mental Disease* 176, 598–606

Marks, I.M. (1981) *Care and Cure of Neurosis*, New York, Wiley

Marks, I.M. (1987) *Fears, Phobias and Rituals*, Oxford, Oxford University Press

Marrazzi, M.A. and Luby, E.D. (1986) An auto-addiction model of chronic anorexia nervosa, *International Journal of Eating Disorders* 5, 191–208

Masson, J. (1992) The tyranny of psychotherapy. In W. Dryden and C. Feltham, *Psychotherapy and its Discontents*, Milton Keynes, Open University Press

Meichenbaum, D.H. (1976) Towards a cognitive therapy of self control. In G. Schwartz and D. Shapiro (eds) *Consciousness and Self Regulation: Advances in Research*, New York, Plenum

Miller, E. (1999) Conversion hysteria: is it a viable concept? *Cognitive Neuropsychiatry* 4, 181–92

Milo, T.J, Kaufman, G.E, Barnes, W., Konopa, L.M., Crayton, J.W., Ringlestein, J.G. and Shirazi, P.H. (2001) Changes in regional blood flow after electro-convulsive therapy for depression, *Journal of ECT* 17, 15–21

Minuchin, S., Rosman, B. and Baker, L. (1978) *Psychosomatic Families: Anorexia Nervosa in Context*, Cambridge MA, Harvard University Press

Mohr, D.C. (1995) Negative outcome in psychotherapy: a critical review, *Clinical Psychology:*

Science and Practice 2, 1–27

Morton, R. (1694) *Phthisiologia; or, a Treatise of Consumptions* (trans. from original 1689 Latin edition in 1694)

Mowrer, O.H. (1939) A stimulus response analysis of anxiety and its role as a reinforcing agent, *Psychological Review* 46, 553–65

Nash, E.H, Hoehn-Saric, R., Battle, C.C., Stone, A.R., Imber, S.D. and Frank, J.D. (1965) Systematic preparation of patients for short term psychotherapy. Relation to characteristics of patient, therapist and the psychotherapeutic process, *Journal of Nervous and Mental Disorders* 140, 374–83

Newark, C.S., Frerking, R.A., Cook, L. and Newmark, I. (1973) Endorsement of Ellis' irrational beliefs as a function of psychopathology, *Journal of Clinical Psychology* 29, 300–2

Ng, C., Schweitzer, I., Alexopolous, P., Celi, E., Wong, L., Tuckwell, V., Sergejew, A. and Tiller, J. (2000) Efficacy and cognitive effects of right unilateral electro-convulsive therapy, *Journal of ECT* 16, 370–9

Ogden, J. (1992) *Fat Chance: The myth of Dieting Explained*, London and New York, Routledge

Parsons, T. (1951) *The Social System*, Glencoe IL, Free Press

Paul, G.L. (1981) Social learning program (with token economy) for adult psychiatric inpatients, *Clinical Psychologist*

Paul, G.L. (1966) *Insight vs Desensitisation in Psychotherapy*, Stanford CA, Stanford University Press

Paul, G.L. and Lentz, R.J. (1977) *Psychosocial Treatment of Chronic Mental Patients: Milieu Versus Social Learning Programs*, Cambridge MA, Harvard University Press

Pedersen, P.B. (1987) *Handbook of Cross Cultural Counselling*, New York, Praeger

Phillips, R.D. (1985) The adjustment of men and women. Mental health professionals' views today, *Academic Psychology Bulletin* 7(2) 253–60

Pickering, J. (1981) Perception. In Psychological Processes, Units 5, 6 and 7, Milton Keynes, Open University Press

Pilgrim, D. (2000) Psychiatric diagnosis: more questions than answers, *The Psychologist* 13(6) 302–5

Pinel, P. (1962) *A Treatise on Insanity* (pub. 1801 in English) (trans. D.D. Davis), New York, Hafner

Price, J. (1968) The genetics of depressed behaviour. In A. Coppen and S. Walk (eds) *Recent Development in the Affective Disorders*, Special Publication No. 2, *British Journal of Psychiatry*

Ralph, R.O. and Kidder, K.A. (2000) *Can We Measure Recovery? A Compendium of Recovery Related Measures*, Cambridge MA, Human Services Research Institute

Rogers, C. (1951) *Client Centred Therapy: Its Current Practice, Implications and Theory*, Boston, Houghton Mifflin

Rogers, C. and Dymond, R.F. (eds) (1954) *Psychotherapy and Personality Change: Co-ordinated Research Studies in the Client Centred Approach*, Chicago, University of Chicago Press

Romme, M. and Escher, S. (2000) *Making Sense of Voices*, London, MIND

Rosenhan, D.L. (1973) On being sane in insane places, *Science* 179, 250–8

Rosenthal, R. and Jacobson, L. (1968) *Pygmalion in the Classroom: Teacher Expectation and Pupils' Intellectual Development*, New York, Holt

Rowan, A. (2002) *Bulimia Nervosa*, London, EDA

Sabin, J.E. (1975) Translating despair, *American Journal of Psychiatry* 132, 197–9

SANE (2002) *Anxiety, Phobia and Obsession*, London, SANE Publications

Scheff, T.J. (1966) *Being Mentally Ill: A Sociological Theory*, Chicago, Aldine

Seligman, M.E. (1974) Depression and learned helplessness. In R.J. Friedman and M.M. Katz (eds) *The Psychology of Depression: Contemporary Theory and Research*, Washington DC, Winston Wiley

Shepherd, G. (1998) Models of community care, *Journal of Mental Health* 7, 165–77

Slater, E. and Shields, J. (1969) Genetic aspects of anxiety. In M.H. Lader (ed.) *Studies of Anxiety*, Ashford, Headley Brothers

Sloane, R.B., Staple, F.R., Cristol, A.H., Yorkston, N.J.

and Whipple, K. (1975) *Psychotherapy Versus Behaviour Therapy*, Cambridge MA, Harvard University Press

Smith, K.A., Fairburn, C.G. and Cowen, P.J. (1999) Symptomatic relapse in bulimia nervosa following acute trytophan depletion, *Archives of General Psychiatry* 56, 171–6

Stein, C.J. and Test, M.A. (1980) Alternative to mental hospital treatment program and clinical evaluation, *Archives of General Psychiatry* 37, 392–7

Steinberg, D. (1989) *Interprofessional Consultation. Innovation and Imagination in Working Relationships*, Oxford, Blackwell Scientific Publications

Stevens, J.R. (1982) Neurology and neuropathology of schizophrenia. In F.A. Henn and G.A. Nasrallah (eds) *Schizophrenia as a Brain Disease*, New York, Oxford University Press

Stirling, J.D. and Hellewell, J.S.E. (1999) *Psychopathology*, London and New York, Routledge

Strober, M., Lampert, C., Morrell, W., Burroughs, J. and Jacobs, C. (1990) A controlled family study of anorexia nervosa, *International Journal of Eating Disorders* 9, 239–53

Sullivan, H.S. (1929) Research in schizophrenia, *American Journal of Psychiatry* 9, 533–67

Sullivan, H.S. (1953) *The Interpersonal Theory of Psychiatry*, New York, Norton

Syal, R. (1997) Doctors find pick-me-up for SAD people, *Sunday Times*, 19 January, 4

Szasz, T. (1960) The myth of mental illness, *American Psychologist* 15, 113–18

Szasz, T. (1962) *The Myth of Mental Illness*, New York, Harper & Row

Taylor, J. (1992) A questionable treatment, *Nursing Times* 88, 41–3

Terman, M. (1988) On the question of mechanism in phototherapy for seasonal affective disorder: considerations of clinical efficacy and epidemiology, *Journal of Biological Rhythms* 3, 155–72

Temerlin, M.K. (1970) Diagnostic bias in community mental health, *Community Mental Health Journal* 6, 110–17

Teuting, P., Rosen, S. and Hirschfield, R. (1981) *Special Report on Depression Research*, Washington DC, NIMH-DHHS publication No. 81-1085

Thompson, L.W., Gallagher, D. and Raab, G.M. (1995) Comparison of effectiveness of psychotherapies, *Journal of Consulting and Clinical Psychology*, 385–90

Torrey, E.F. (1988) *Surviving Schizophrenia*, revised edition, New York, Harper & Row

Touyz, S.W., Beaumont, P.J.V., Glaun, D., Phillips, T. and Cowie, I. (1984) A comparison of lenient and strict operant conditioning programmes in refeeding patients with anorexia nervosa, *British Journal of Psychiatry* 144, 517–20

Ullman, L.P. and Krasner, L. (1969) *A Psychological Approach to Abnormal Behaviour*, Englewood Cliffs NJ, Prentice Hall

Ussher, J. (1989) *Acknowledging Gender Issues in Clinical Psychology*, Clinical Psychology Forum

Ussher, J. (1991) *Women's Madness: Misogyny or Mental Illness?* Harvester Wheatsheaf

van den Brouke, S., Vandereycken, W. and Vertommen, H. (1995) Marital communications in eating disorders, *International Journal of Eating Disorders* 17, 1–23

Wachtel, P.L. (1977) *Psychoanalysis and Behaviour Therapy: Towards an Integration*, New York, Basic Books

Walker, M. (1994) *Women in Counselling and Therapy*, Milton Keynes, Open University Press

Watson, J.B. and Rayner, R. (1920) Conditioned emotional reactions, *Journal of Experimental Psychology* 3, 1–14

Weissman, A.N. and Beck, A.T. (1978) Development and validation of the dysfunctional attitude scale: a preliminary investigation. Paper presented at the annual meeting of the American Educational Research Association, Toronto

Weissman, M.M. and Klerman, G. (1977) Sex differences and the epidemiology of depression, *Archives of General Psychiatry* 34, 98–117

Whittal, M.I., Agras, S.W. and Gould, R.A. (1999) Bulimia nervosa. A meta analysis of psychosocial and pharmacological treatments, *Behaviour Therapy* 30, 117–35

Whittel, G. (1995) Spectacular northern lights linked to suicidal depression, *Times*, 15 April, 9

Wolpe, J. (1958) *Psychotherapy by Reciprocal Inhibition*, Stanford CA, Stanford University Press

Wolpe, J. (1973) *The Practice of Behaviour Therapy*, New York, Pergamon Press

Woodside, D.B., Shekter-Wolfson, L.F., Garfinkel, P.F. and Olmsted, M.P. (1995) Family interactions in bulimia nervosa. Study design, comparisons to established population norms and changes over the course of an intensive day hospital treatment program, *International Journal of Eating Disorders* 17, 105–15

World Health Organization (1979) *Schizophrenia: An International Follow up Study*, Geneva, Wiley

Youssef, H.A. and Youssef, F.A. (1999) Time to abandon electroconvulsion as a treatment in modern psychiatry, *Advances in Therapy* 16(1)

Yun, Z., Jumian, X., Wang, X. and Jiang, K. (1997) A study of cognitions and body sensations in anxiety disorders, *Acat Psychologica Sinica* 29, 60–6

Zellner, D.A., Harer, D.E. and Adler, R.L. (1989) Effects of eating abnormalities and gender perceptions of desirable body shape, *Journal of Abnormal Psychology* 98, 93–6

Index